MARINES
AT WAR

MARINES AT WAR

IAN DEAR

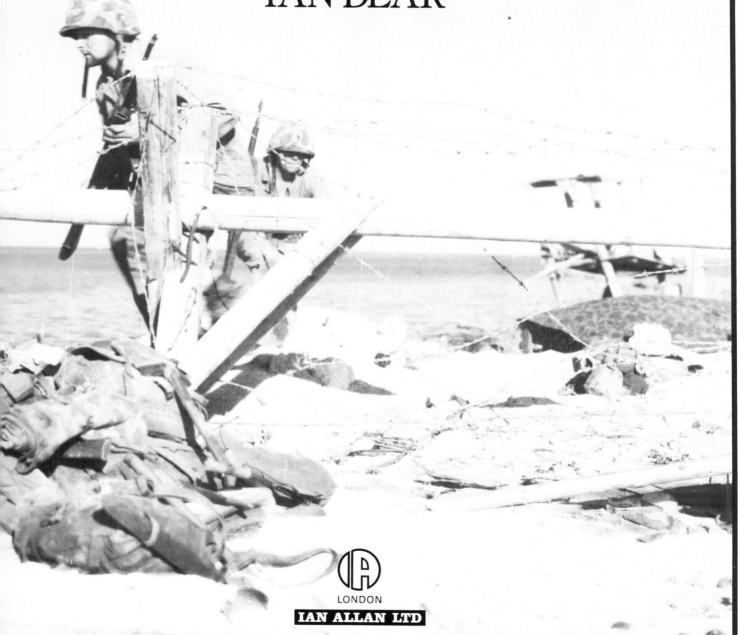

IA
LONDON
IAN ALLAN LTD

First published 1982

ISBN 0 7110 1147 8

© Ian Dear 1982

Published by Ian Allan Ltd, Shepperton, Surrey;
and printed by Ian Allan Printing Ltd at their works
at Coombelands in Runnymede, England

Contents

Introduction

The essence of marines, to whichever nation they belong and wherever they serve, is that they are as much at home fighting at sea as they are on the land. *Per Mare Per Terram* is the motto of the British Royal Marines.

This book does not pretend to encompass the history of all the brave deeds of the many maritime regiments around the world. What it does do is focus on some of the most memorable amphibious operations in which the US Marine Corps and the Royal Marines were involved during World War 2. By doing this I hope to show the true amphibious nature of marines everywhere, and their flexibility as a fighting force. I have, however, made two exceptions to this; the defence of Wake Island and a brief description of the

Royal Marines Siege Regiment. I have described these because they were unique and because they show in action, in both cases, the marine corps of two nations in a time of adversity, and how these corps responded with a tremendous will to fight on in any circumstances and to adapt to these circumstances with ingenuity and determination.

In the United States the marine corps is an elite force which during World War 2 had — and still has — its own air arm, artillery, tank regiments, and so on. The British marines, on the other hand, though equally prestigious, has always been a very much smaller force which during World War 2 had none, or virtually none, of these supporting

arms. Another great difference between the two corps is the number of men who were involved in the different campaigns I have described. With the Royal Marines, only a few thousand were in action at any one time. Force Viper, for instance, a typically amphibious role for sea soldiers, numbered only about a hundred men. On the other hand no less than 60,000 men of the US Marine Corps took part in one of the biggest amphibious landings ever planned when they swarmed ashore at Iwo Jima. But I have chosen to write about both because though very different in size, concept and achievement the one thing that binds them together is not only the amphibious nature of both operations but the bravery, resourcefulness and sheer tenacity of the participants. These are virtues that also rank high in the other battles I have described, and even after 35 years no one can possibly read about Tarawa or Walcheren without marvelling at the bravery of the men who took part in them.

I wish there was room to describe the many other activities in which the marines of both nations were involved between 1939 and 1945: the flyers of the US Marine Aviation Wing and the Royal Marines who flew with the British Fleet Air Arm; the large number of marines of both nations who manned the armaments of warships, and the daring raids of small units like the Raiders Battalion at Makin or Col Hasler's canoe sortie on enemy shipping at Bordeaux. But by concentrating on the amphibious nature of marines I believe I am reflecting their modern role. They really are soldiers of the sea who can, when the occasion demands it, fly a combat aircraft, man a coastal gun, a ship's turret, or an anti-aircraft battery; ski, swim, or parachute into combat; or simply, with a rifle and bayonet, show they are the best fighting force in the world.

It is impossible to mention by name all the many members or the Royal Marines and the US Marine Corps who were of such enormous help to me in compiling accurate descriptions of the various operations, but I would like to thank, most warmly, the Commandant-General, Royal Marines, Lt-Gen Sir Steuart Pringle Bt, Maj-Gen R.N. Thomas RM, Maj-Gen J. L. Moulton RM and Col J. E. Greenwood USMC, for their assistance and advice, and mention must be given to the staffs of the Royal Marine Museum at Eastney, the History and Museums Division of the US Marine Corps, and the Library and photographic department of the Imperial War Museum, all of whom were unfailingly courteous and generous with their time.

These sulphur fumes at the northern end of Iwo Jima stank like rotten eggs. The two marines have take up a defensive position in a destroyed 5in Japanese gun emplacement. *USMC*

The RM Siege Regiment

The Royal Marines have always been involved with shore artillery as well as with naval guns at sea. When the Battle of Britain started in the summer of 1940 both the heavy and light anti-aircraft batteries of the 1st Mobile Naval Base Defence Organisation (MNBDO 1) were posted to Dover and acquitted themselves with distinction. Later in the war similar units were in action defending London and Antwerp against the flying bomb, and, in an artillery role, helping to clear the Germans from the banks of the Scheldt River. But in their role of gunners ashore the Royal Marines are almost certainly best remembered during World War 2 as the originators of the RM Siege Regiment.

The Royal Marine Siege Regiment was formed in July 1940 on the direct orders of the Prime Minister, Winston Churchill. Commanded by Maj Fellowes RM, the Siege Regiment quickly acquired two 14in siege guns and, later, three 13.5in railway guns,

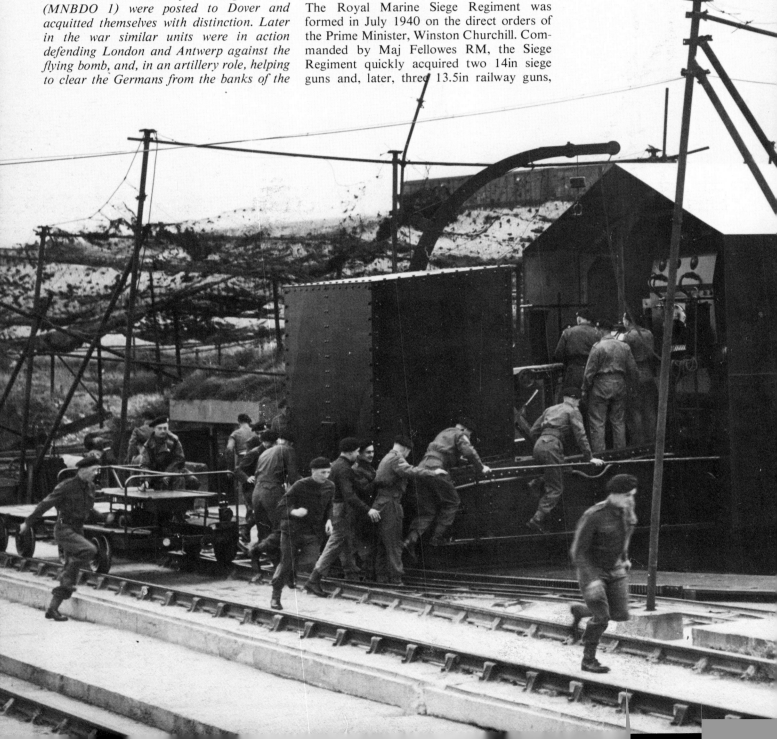

and these were employed in firing across the English Channel at enemy gun emplacements and at Calais where, in the summer of 1940, the German invasion barges were being concentrated.

The gun to be acquired by the Siege Regiment was christened 'Winnie' after the Prime Minister. A spare 14in gun from the battleship HMS *Howe*, it fired the Regiment's first shot from its emplacement on the 12th green of St Margaret's Golf Club on 22 August 1940 when it engaged German batteries in the Cap Griz Nez area to cover the passage of an allied convoy. It was the first shell ever fired from England to France.

A second 14in gun, nicknamed 'Pooh', was installed in December 1940, and later

three World War 1 railway mountings were found and were married to three 13.5in naval guns of the 'Iron Duke' class. The three 13.5in guns should have been destroyed under the terms of the Washington Treaty, but were quickly put to use after being found in an ordnance depot at Nottingham. Once mounted they were taken to the Dover area and joined the Siege Regiment, where they ran on special spurs of railway line custom built for them up to the top of the cliffs. These lines ran back to several cuttings and tunnels inland where the guns were hidden when not in use. The guns' recoil was taken up by running back on these lines and a small diesel engine would then push them back to their firing positions. Because a super-charge

Action Stations! 'Winnie' being manned. *RM Archives*

Right: 'Winnie' being off-loaded from the travelling gun set with the help of three 50ton cranes. *RM Archives*

Below: Front view of 'Winnie'. *RM Archives*

Bottom: Fire! *RM Archives*

was used to get the range required, the gun crew would seek shelter before firing a gun by means of a long lanyard.

'Winnie' and 'Pooh' also used super-charges. The normal 14in HE nose-fused shell was employed but the charge of cordite was increased from the normal 400lb to 485lb. This gave the guns a range of 40,000yds (22.72 miles) but it produced excessive wear, and after the guns had fired 50 rounds the barrels had to be replaced as the shells were no longer able to reach France.

In 1942 work was started on a 'hyper-velocity' long-range gun and after some experimenting an 8in liner was fitted into a 13.5in gun. The liner was made as long as the existing machinery could make it and it stuck out quite a distance beyond the muzzle of the gun. However, the arrangement worked satisfactorily and when tested fired a 250lb shell the incredible distance of 57 miles. Two of these 'hyper-velocity' guns were made and the second was allotted to the Siege Regiment. It was nicknamed 'Bruce' after Adm Sir Bruce Fraser who originated the idea and when it was test-fired on 30 March 1943 it achieved the remarkable range of over 62 miles. Unfortunately, 'Bruce' also became a victim of excessive wear and after 30 shots was not used again.

By the end of 1942 the risk of invasion had faded and the Siege Regiment was reduced to battery strength and the railway guns were handed over to the Home Guard. But 'Winnie' and 'Pooh', despite being hampered by inadequate aerial observation, kept firing

Above: The Operations Room.
RM Archives

Left: The shell wagon; the
ammunition was kept in railway
wagons. *RM Archives*

11

and when in September 1944 the Canadians were closing in on Boulogne and the Cap Griz Nez peninsula, a spotter aircraft was lent to the battery enabling it to fire with great accuracy on German batteries and mobile guns in these areas. On 17 September 1944 the battery fired 174 shells at the Battery Lindemann and two days later it engaged the Battery Grosser Kurfürst obtaining 25 hits. The day after that it obtained six direct hits on the Battery Todt, but on 30 September all the German batteries were overrun and the work of the RM Siege Regiment was at an end.

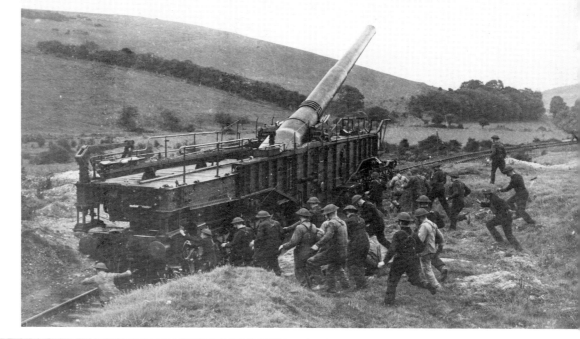

Left: 'Pooh'. *RM Archives*

Below left: Rear view of 'Pooh'. *RM Archives*

Right: The crew of one of the 13.5in railway guns closing up to reload. *RM Archives*

Left: Fire! *RM Archives*

Below: How 'Bruce' was constructed.

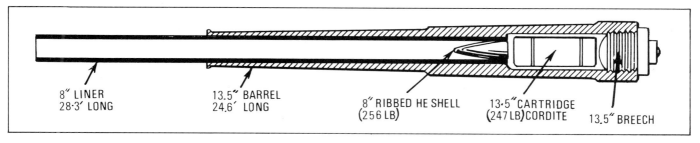

8″ LINER 28·3′ LONG   13.5″ BARREL 24.6′ LONG   8″ RIBBED HE SHELL (256 LB)   13·5″ CARTRIDGE (247 LB) CORDITE   13.5″ BREECH

Wake Island

To Americans the defence of Wake in December 1941 was what the marines were all about: staunch defenders in the face of an overwhelmingly superior enemy force, hard fighters hard to kill.

Wake was a remote atoll, a dot in the vast Pacific some 2,000 miles west of Honolulu. Because of its position it was a vital outpost for the Americans, an invaluable base for patrol planes, a finger pointing at the heart of the potential enemy, the Japanese. So it was not surprising that a few hours after they struck at Pearl Harbor without warning, the Japanese started their attack on Wake.

In April 1941 the C-in-C Pacific Fleet, Adm Kimmel, had recommended that Wake be fortified. As a result of this recommendation work was started on civil and military installations including an airstrip and a seaplane base, and a detachment from the 1st Marine Defense Battalion was established on the three islands, Wake, Wilkes and Peale, that made up Wake Atoll. The detachment was under the command of Maj James Devereux while overall command of the island was in the hands of a naval commander, Winfield S. Cunningham. The detachment, totalling 15 officers and 373

Wake Atoll from the air while being bombed by Liberators in 1944.
US Marine Corps (USMC)

men, controlled four 3in AA batteries and three 5in coastal batteries but otherwise had only 0.3in and 0.50in machine guns and their personal weapons. Although all the marines in the detachment had been trained initially as infantrymen — and so this role was not foreign to them — they were on Wake as specialists, something worth remembering when reading of their heroic defence of the atoll. In addition to the marines Cdr Cunningham had under his command nine naval officers and 58 ratings, one US Army Air Corps officer and four men, and something over 1,000 civilians who were working on the civilian installations. These civilians played a notable role in the defence of the atoll, over 300 of them actually fighting alongside the service personnel.

Also based on Wake was a Marine Fighter Squadron (VMF-211) consisting of 12 new F4F-3 Grumman Wildcat fighters, 12 officers and 49 men all under the command of Maj Paul A. Putnam. The squadron arrived just three days before the Japanese attacked Pearl Harbor and then Wake, and it was badly hampered by the fact that the airstrip was too narrow to allow more than one aircraft to take off at a time. Additionally, parking facilities were rudimentary, instruction manuals for the new aircraft were non-existent, and there were, in any case, practically no experienced ground staff for maintenance work. To make matters worse the bomb racks on the new aircraft could not accommodate the bombs available on the island, and had to be adapted. Understaffed and unused to their new aircraft the squadron was not in a high state of readiness to counter enemy air strikes.

The ground forces were hardly in any better state, for there were not enough trained crews for the guns. Consequently, one 3in AA battery — F — could not be manned at all (it was in any case without vital equipment), and the other two AA batteries, D and E, could only have three of their four guns manned. E Battery had no

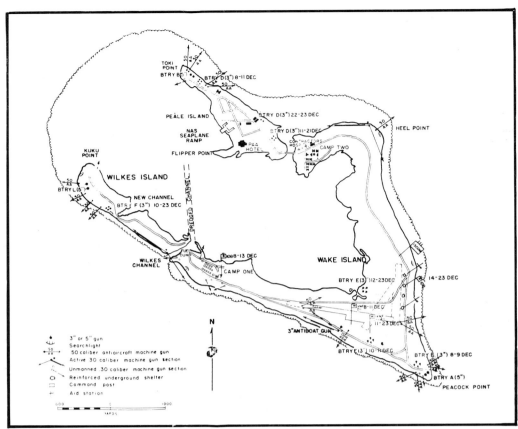

Left: The Defence installations on Wake, December 1941.
Reproduced by kind permission of Historical Branch, USMC

Below: Map of surface action, 11 December.
Reproduced by kind permission of Historical Branch, USMC

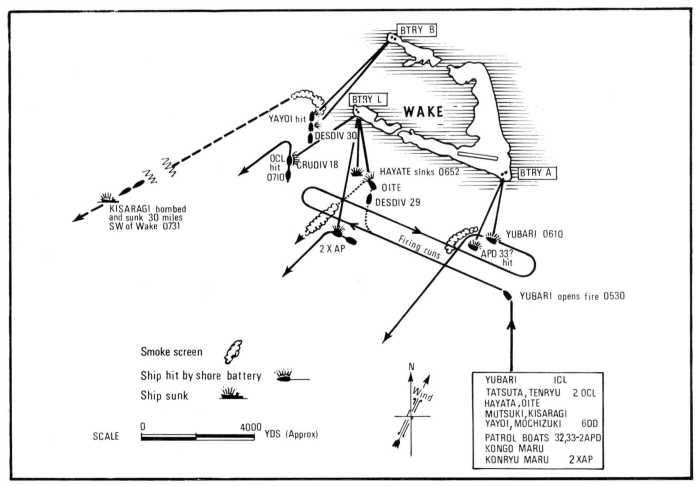

height finder and had to rely on D Battery for this information. The machine guns, both aerial and ground, were also badly under-manned. Only the 5in coastal batteries were up to strength. When the Japanese made their first aerial attack, on Monday 8 December (Sunday 7 December east of the International Date Line), Peale was the most advanced in defence construction, with Wake next and Wilkes a poor third. When the AA batteries went into action against the Japanese bombers it was the first time they had ever been fired by their crews, though the marines had been trained on similar weapons.

The garrison, alerted by signal that Pearl Harbor was under attack, went to action stations, and by 0735 hours all positions were manned. At midday, under cover of a rain squall and the noise of the ever-present surf, the Japanese made their first air-strike with a force of 36 bombers. These were immediately engaged by the AA machine guns, the 3in batteries not being effective against the very low level attacks employed by the bombers. The raid was a disaster for the marines for seven of the Grummans were destroyed on the ground along with a huge quantity of aviation fuel. Worst of all, 55 marine aviation personnel were killed or wounded. At one stroke the squadron had suffered 60% casualties. To add to the squadron's misfortunes one of the four air-craft that had been on patrol at the time of the raid struck debris on landing and was damaged. This only left three aircraft in flying condition, but over the next days miraculous work was done stripping the destroyed aeroplanes and keeping the remainder flying with whatever materials the ground crews managed to find.

This first raid also damaged vital equipment belonging to the coastal batteries and when the bombers returned the next day more damage was inflicted, with the civilian hospital being destroyed and the seaplane base severely damaged. But this time the raiders did not escape unscathed. The air patrol shot down one and the AA batteries destroyed another and damaged several others. Four marines and 55 civilians were killed in this second raid. But from the second day the raids took on a pattern which the Wake defenders were able to recognise and therefore take measures against. The AA batteries, for instance, were obvious enemy targets and so were continually moved.

During these first days, while the Japanese were attacking Wake from the air they were also mustering an invasion force of some 450 men backed by a naval task force of three cruisers, six destroyers, two troop-carrying destroyers and two medium transports. At the same time the Americans, still reeling under the blow of Pearl Harbor, were getting together a relief carrier force for Wake.

On the night of 11 December the enemy task force appeared off Wake, high seas and poor visibility enabling them to escape detection until they were off the atoll. As the enemy warships closed in the marines held their fire, both to hide their positions and to make sure of their targets. Then at 0615 hours, with the Japanese flagship, the cruiser *Yubari*, close to the south shore, the defence batteries opened fire. The *Yubari* was hit almost immediately by A Battery whose commander, Lt Barninger, later reported:

'The first salvo from our guns which hit her was fired at a range of 5,500-6,000 yards, bearing about 180 degrees to 190 degrees. Both shells entered her port side about amidships just above the waterline. The ship immediately belched smoke and steam through the side and her speed diminished. At 7,000 yards two more hit her in about the same place, but more probably slightly aft of the first two. Her whole side was now engulfed in smoke and steam and she turned to starboard again to try and hide in the smoke. At this time the destroyer which had accompanied the cruiser came in at high speed, tried to sweep between us to lay smoke, but a shell, an over, aft of the cruiser, struck the forecastle of the destroyer. This hit was observed by Lt Hanna, .50 calibre machine gun officer from his CP. The destroyer immediately turned, although fire was not directed at her, and fled. We continued to fire on the cruiser and although I am quite certain that we got two more into her side, I could not be sure of it. I am sure of the first four. The only hit I am certain of after this time was a hit on her forward turret. A shell hit the face of the turret and this turret did not fire again . . .

'After we ceased firing, the whole fleet having fled and there being no other targets to engage, the cruiser lay broadside to the sea still pouring steam and smoke from her side. She had a definite port list. After some time she got slowly under way, going a short distance, stopping, and continuing again; she was engulfed in smoke when she crept over the horizon.'

During the whole of this engagement, the *Yubari* returned A Battery's fire and continued to fire long after she had got beyond the range of the battery's guns. However, she only managed to injure one marine, and she ceased fire at 18,000yds.

While A Battery was engaging the *Yubari*, L Battery, positioned on Wilkes Island, found that its field of fire was almost completely filled with enemy vessels. The crew first opened fire at 0650 hours and almost immediately hit the leading destroyer of

three, the *Hayate*, which sank within two minutes, becoming the first enemy surface craft to be sunk by Americans. The marines were so delighted with their accurate gunfire that they stood and cheered instead of training on the next target. It took a battle-hardened veteran, Platoon Sgt Henry Bedell, to bring them to their senses. 'Knock it off you bastards,' he yelled, 'and get back to the guns. What d'ya think this is, a ball game?' Sgt Bedell's rebuke had the desired effect and moments later the battery hit the next destroyer in line, the *Oite*, which, with the remaining destroyer, then turned away. The battery commander, 2-Lt McAlister, checked his battery's fire, and then found a new target. This was the two transports carrying the troops for the invasion of Wake. The battery scored hits on one transport before they too retired behind a smokescreen. Finally, the battery fired on one of the light cruisers scoring a hit before the cruiser turned away from the island. By 0710 hours, after firing 120 rounds, L Battery had no more targets and ceased firing. It had sustained only two casualties, both light.

Further north on Peale Island B Battery had engaged the other half of the destroyer force. At 10,000yds the battery opened fire on the leading vessel. The Japanese returned the fire with great accuracy and a considerable amount of damage was done before the leading destroyer was hit and set on fire. All three warships then retired under cover of a smokescreen.

With the Japanese invasion force now in full retreat the four operational Grummans were sent to harass them, and — with their bomb racks now precariously adapted to take the bombs stored on Wake — the aircraft first bombed and strafed the two light cruisers and then attacked the two transports and the destroyers. The Japanese replied with heavy AA fire but the destroyer *Kisaragi* was seen to blow up and several other enemy ships were damaged before they disappeared over the horizon.

It had been a notable victory for the marines, both on the ground and in the air, but they had hardly had time to celebrate before the Japanese were again attacking, this time from the air with 30 bombers, and the next morning at dawn two Kawanishi patrol flying boats strafed the islands. One was later shot down by one of the remaining operational Grummans.

These attacks from the air continued over the next days, and an extract from the report of B Battery's commander, Capt Godbold, describes well how the marines fought off these assaults while at the same time trying to improve their defensive positions.

'0700 Continued work on large personnel shelter during day. Height finder shelter completed.

1300 One of our fighters reported enemy bombers approaching island from the east at altitude of 18,000ft. 18 bombers in two formations of nine planes each attacked the island. Battery fired 95 rounds. Four planes were smoking heavily as they left the island. One enemy plane was observed crashing into the ocean some distance from the island. Bombs fell in lagoon near battery.

1800 Island attacked by one patrol plane. Bombs fell across road from battery position. Battery position heavily machine-gunned. Due to low visibility, battery did not fire.

1900 Set night watch. 75-man working party completed large personnel shelter. Pfc L. N. Schneider and Pvt A. LePore reported for duty from the Marine garage.'

The continuous air attacks caused casualties, destroyed vital range-finding equipment and incapacitated all but two of the Grummans, and on 21 December D Battery was virtually destroyed. Then on the morning of 22 December the last two Grummans were destroyed while in action against the Japanese bombers and Wake was without any air defence. What remained of the squadron — 20 officers and enlisted men — became infantry, and plans were drawn up for the marines manning the batteries to assume this role as well when the invasion force returned — as it inevitably would —

and once their battery guns had ceased to be of use.

While the Japanese hammered away at the atoll from the air they were also patching up and reinforcing their invasion fleet, and before dawn on 23 December 1,500 men of the Japanese Special Navy Landing Force — the Japanese marines — embarked in destroyer-transports and swarmed ashore on the south coast of Wake Island near the air-strip after their transports had been deliberately run aground. The main force landed in this manner, but there were landings elsewhere as well. Confused fighting took place in the dark but by first light the Japanese had consolidated their landing and were pushing north up the east leg of Wake Island and west towards Wilkes Island. This latter force surrounded the marine aviation personnel who had been deployed to defend a 3in AA gun manned by some of Lt Hanna's men. This gun, although it could only be aimed by being sighted through the bore, had caused the invasion force some damage and had set alight one of the beached transports. Fierce fighting developed around it.

At 0500 hours Cdr Cunningham sent the following signal: 'Enemy on island — issue in doubt.' East of Camp One a defensive line had been established by Maj Devereux and he put 2-Lt Poindexter in charge of assembling all available personnel along it. Another defensive line, under Devereux's Executive Officer, Maj Potter, was established south of the Command Post to defend the road north and Devereux called on Capt Godbold to move south with all available personnel to reinforce this line.

By 0700 hours it became clear that the position of the tiny marine force and its helpers was desperate. All communications with Wilkes Island had been cut but B Battery on Peale reported seeing Japanese flags flying all over the island, and it was therefore presumed — erroneously — that the island had already fallen to the enemy. Maj Potter's line, no more than a platoon in strength, was hopelessly overextended, and though Lt Poindexter's line east of Camp One was in a stronger position it was driven on to the defensive and had no opportunity to counter-attack. In the south-east corner of Wake Island A Battery's commander had thrown a defence perimeter around his guns and was holding off the enemy as were the remnants of VMF-211 which fought off several hundred Japanese for six hours until all the defenders of the 3in AA gun, which included several civilians, were either killed or wounded.

As the morning progressed it became obvious that the marines could not hold out for much longer. Those who looked out to sea in the hope of seeing a relief force saw only a ring of Japanese warships. Further off beyond the horizon the two Japanese carriers *Soryo* and *Hiryu* were preparing to launch their planes to bomb and strafe the Wake defenders into submission. Maj Devereux reported to Cdr Cunningham on the seriousness of the situation and asked if any relief was expected. Cdr Cunningham replied in the negative for he now knew that the American High Command, fearing for the safety of the precious carriers, had abandoned any attempt to relieve Wake, and at 0800 hours he decided that the only course left open to him was to surrender.

What neither Devereux nor Cunningham knew was that the Wilkes Island detachment of some 70 marines had not surrendered but were in the process of vigorously opposing the force of about 100 Japanese which had landed right by F Battery. Soon a hand-to-hand battle was in progress around its emplacement but when it became obvious that the battery could not be held against the superior enemy force the guns were disabled and the battery personnel fell back to the eastern part of the island and joined up with marines from L Battery who had managed to establish a defensive position under Lt McAlister near the channel that divided Wilkes and Wake islands. When the Japanese force tried to move westwards to take L Battery they were pinned down by one of the 0.50in AA machine guns which kept up accurate and damaging fire on them while Capt Platt, L Battery's commander, moved out from his command post on the far side of the island, gathered a small party of two machine gun crews and eight riflemen, and moved east towards F Battery to attack the Japanese whom he could see now occupied the gun emplacement. The assault took the enemy completely by surprise and they were driven back towards the line established by Lt McAlister's party. Caught between these two forces the Japanese were eliminated. 94 bodies were counted, four of them officers.

During the next hours, as Capt Platt tried vainly to contact Maj Devereux, the tiny marine force on Wilkes was heavily shelled and strafed by the Japanese. Then, at about 1300 hours, Maj Devereux was seen approaching the channel that divided the two islands accompanied by a Japanese officer, and Capt Platt was told that the atoll had been surrendered to the Japanese.

With extraordinary courage a small force of marines, bravely supported by a considerable number of civilians, had taken on the might of Japan and had sunk four enemy warships, destroyed 21 of its aircraft, and killed upwards of 1,000 Japanese troops.

Below: The smashed remains of VMF-211. *USMC*

Right: The Stars and Stripes are hoisted over Wake again. The Japanese garrison salute. *USMC*

This was the landing point across which it was intended to ferry all personnel, tanks, guns and W/T of the Burma Army! *RM Archives*

Force Viper

Early in 1942 when the Japanese were still advancing unchecked towards India a small volunteer force of Royal Marines was raised from a detachment in Ceylon to patrol the Gulf of Martaban to prevent the outflanking of the 17th Indian Division defending the approaches to Rangoon. The idea was to prevent Japanese troops infiltrating behind the British lines on rafts. To counter this the marines were to patrol the east coast of the gulf but by the time they arrived Moulmein was already lost and the 17th Division was falling back on the Sittang River.

The force of five officers and 102 other ranks that arrived in Rangoon on 11 February 1942 was called 'Force Viper' by its commander, Maj Duncan Johnston, after a venomous British snake. He wanted, he said, to 'bite the enemy hard'. Armed with Bren guns, Tommy guns, 2in mortars and a Vickers Type K anti-aircraft gun, the marines arrived in the British cruiser HMS *Enterprise* on what was to become one of the strangest tasks in retreat ever undertaken by the Royal Marines.

The loss of Moulmein, however, left the force temporarily without a job but on 18 February Johnston was ordered to form a flotilla for river work. It took him two days to find the river craft he needed but with the help of two local Europeans who joined Force Viper, Lt Penman and Sub-Lt Wikner, both of the Burma RNVR, four government touring launches (*Doris, Rita, Stella* and *Delta*) complete with their native crews, and two diesel motor boats, *Ngagin* and *Ngagyi*, were acquired.

By this time the Japanese were nearing Rangoon and on 20 February Johnston was ordered to take his small force to nearby Syriam and defend the oil refineries there. When they arrived there the force found that the police had already been evacuated and so they took on the additional task of maintaining law and order in the area. On 4 March, after some hurried training on the new craft, Force Viper started patrolling the Rangoon and Pegu rivers, including the Rangoon waterfront where looters were to be shot on sight. Then, three days later, orders for the evacuation of Rangoon came through and the force was given the task of evacuating the demolition parties instructed to destroy the oil refineries at Syriam, Seikgyi and Thilawa, and then to make their way 100 miles upriver to Prome. The refineries were destroyed — in one alone 20 million gallons of aviation spirit went up in a pall of black smoke — and amidst the turmoil and confusion that always surround an evacuation, Force Viper slipped away up the Irrawaddy to Prome.

When Johnston and his men arrived at Prome on 13 March they were put under the command of the 17th Indian Division which was fighting the Japanese north of Tharrawan. Johnston was ordered to protect the division's right flank by preventing enemy vessels coming up the river or crossing it. The two motor boats were now returned to their owners, the Irrawaddy Flotilla Company, and were replaced by two armoured kerosene motor boats, *Xylia* and *Delta Guard 9*. Never before could the White Ensign have flown on such a curious collection of craft, but even odder ones were pressed into service later on. Patrols were instituted down-river as far as Henzada, and

Left: Rangoon burning. Note the Vickers type K anti-aircraft gun. *RM Archives*

Centre left: The demolition party returns to *Stella* while in the background the Syriam oil refinery burns. Maj Johnson has his back to the camera and his hands on his hips. *RM Archives*

Right: Landing party going ashore. *RM Archives*

Below: A patrol boat taking a large country boat in tow. *RM Archives*

Above: Harry, surely one of the strangest craft ever to fly the white ensign. *RM Archives*

Left: Rita returning from patrol with a signalman on the wheelhouse roof. *RM Archives*

were deliberately varied by Johnston. Sometimes one boat would go down, followed by another, sometimes they would all go down together, and occasionally none would go.

As the days passed the water in the river dropped and it became increasingly difficult to navigate. The launches often ran aground and pro-Japanese Burmans did not improve the situation when they started to remove the buoyage system. The enemy harassed them frequently with mortar fire from the dense jungle, and occasionally from the air.

On 22 March Johnston heard that the enemy were moving towards Myanaung from Henzada and so he based himself at Myanaung keeping the next town, Kanaung, six miles downstream, under observation. On the same day, Lt-Col Musgrave, commanding officer of 2 Burma Commando, which had been formed from members of the Bush Warfare School at Maymo, took over general command of Force Viper and for the next week or so army commandos and Royal Marines fought side by side.

It was soon discovered that the Japanese were by-passing Myanaung and were due to arrive by the banks of the Irrawaddy 10 miles north, at Kyangin. Musgrave decided to move upriver and lay an ambush. His force for this operation consisted of No 2 Commando, the RM Vickers gun section and No 2 Platoon of Force Viper, and a company of the Burma Military Police which had turned up a few days previously. The flotilla ferried this force upstream and after some delay caused by some of the boats running aground, the force arrived at dusk. On their arrival they were told that both Kansung and Myanaung had fallen. 'In both towns', Johnston commented, 'the Home Guard, a body with flashy uniforms and vague duties, had formed the reception committee to welcome the enemy', and there is no doubt that the Burmese were of little help in trying to repel the invading Japanese. The ambush was laid but by the next morning it became apparent that the enemy had by-passed Kyangin and were heading north, and Musgrave therefore re-embarked his force and moved up-river to Padaung eight miles below Prome, which he was ordered to hold against the advancing enemy. By the time the force arrived there the 17th Indian Division were heavily

25

engaged at Shivedaung, opposite Padaung, and there was a tank battle in progress.

No 2 platoon under Lt Fayle RM formed the force's reserve and it was positioned near Musgrave's HQ which was set up in a bungalow standing in a compound. The Vickers section was positioned at a crossroads near the compound to cover the open ground inland. Commando patrols reported no enemy north of Tonbo 18 miles to the south of Force Viper so the force settled down for the night not expecting any trouble until the next day. But at 0030 hours Johnston was woken by a burst of Tommy gun fire in the compound and it later transpired that, although perfectly friendly when the force had entered the village, the inhabitants had concealed a force of Japanese in their houses. Johnston reported:
'The Colonel, Fayle and I dashed down to see what was happening. There was bright moonlight, and the compound was quiet, except for a subdued scuffling going on outside. I went out on the road, and saw figures quietly crossing towards the compound further down. Ten yards from me a figure was kneeling on the road, and another lying on the edge of it. I had a good look at him, and decided he was a Jap. I fired a revolver shot at him, but missed, and jumped behind a latrine. I told the Colonel they were definitely Japs. Meanwhile, the far corner of the compound, nearest the river, was filling up with troops. The Colonel and I got all the reserve platoon that we could see, and sprinted 50 yards down the road to where it crossed a dry gulley. As we went, there was a yell from the Japs, and Tommies, automatic weapons, and rifles opened fire. I had lost touch with Fayle. We took up positions along the gulley, and fired back into the compound, which was now seething with troops. After a little while we were fired on from behind as well as in front, and the air was thick with bullets. Our ammunition began to run out. One Bren had none left, another had only one magazine. There was no hope of contacting Cave's platoon in the melee, and the Colonel decided we should beat it.'

They scrambled back along the gulley, over some paddy fields and then headed back to the flotilla moored some six miles upstream where they were later joined by Fayle and the rest of his platoon, but neither the Vickers section nor Cave's platoon were seen again. At the time Johnston assumed Cave had made for the hills as ordered and that the Vickers section had been overpowered. But eventually, when Cave's platoon failed to reappear, it was thought that it too had been wiped out, and all were subsequently reported 'missing believed killed'.

However, a handful of Cave's platoon did survive after spending some years in captivity, and one of them later described the platoon's ordeal:
'When the Jap attack got under way we seemed at first to be some distance away from the action. Lt Cave decided that we attempt to return to our temporary HQ as the action appeared to be in that direction. We moved off but almost ran foul of what sounded like a large body of Japs between us and Padaung. Lt Cave then took us towards the hills as instructed. We went as best we could till dawn, when Lt Cave decided we should lie low by day, or for part of the day at least. There was the sound of fighting on three sides of us by now but at a considerable distance from us. We were also lost by now, Lt Cave having damaged his compass.'

After several encounters with the enemy which reduced the platoon to 10 marines — all of whom by this time were in bad condition — and three Gurkhas they had found in the jungle, Cave and his men ran into a strong force of Japanese at Toungoo, between Prome and Alanmyo. A member of the platoon wrote:
'We came under mortar and heavy machine gun fire from the front and to our right. The machine gun seemed closer than the mortar and several times we thought we heard Jap voices. We returned the fire in the direction of the machine gun, as this was harassing us more than the mortar which wasn't very accurate. The Gurkha Lance Naik

Below: The flotilla moves north after the bombing and machine gunning of Yenangyoung. *RM Archives*

Right: Mountain battery transport being embarked for the trip across the Chindwin. *RM Archives*

Below right: The second ferrying operation at Shwegyn. *RM Archives*

Right: Ferrying troops across the Chindwin. Note the lowness of the river as shown by the opposite bank. *RM Archives*

Below: On the Irrawaddy going north to Prome. The flotilla make fast to one another for distribution of rations. *RM Archives*

volunteered to Cave to go out at dusk with one of his men and try to silence the machine gun and at dusk they slipped out of the position. The rest of us said a mental goodbye to them. After what seemed an age we heard a burst of yelling, one shot, and then silence. The two Gurkhas slipped back into the position near dawn, the Lance Naik telling Cave excitedly that the gun crew were dead and the gun out of action. The two Gurkhas then each displayed two human ears on a cord to prove that they had really done the job'.

The next day Cave was wounded in the knee by a mortar fragment and the small force was surrounded. Eventually the Japanese burst from dense cover on the party's left flank, and a larger party charged them from the rear. All one of the survivors can remember is Cave yelling 'Into the bastards boys, we're Royal Marines', before a blow on the head knocked him out. The force was captured complete and put in a POW camp at Mogok. There Cave died and by the time the remnants of the platoon were rescued by Chinese forces under Gen 'Vinegar Joe' Stilwell only five marines remained alive, though two died in India soon after their release.

When the Japanese attack on the compound came, Lt Fayle had been luckier than Cave. By the time the colonel had given the order to retreat from the compound, Fayle had become detached from his platoon and had slipped under the police huts in the compound which were raised about three feet off the ground. With him were Cpl Winters, with a rifle, and Marine Shaw with a Bren gun. Fayle had armed himself with a Tommy gun and grenades. These three opened fire at short range on the Japanese troops massing in the compound. The enemy then tried to rush them, but without success. An officer then stood up and told them to lay down their arms or be shot, but Shaw shot him. Again the enemy tried to rush them and again they failed.

As the moon was now getting low the three marines moved to another hut to keep

27

Viper by 35 men and one officer, about one-third of its strength, but all the launches, with the exception of *Delta Guard 9*, were kept operational and on 31 March *Stella* was sent upstream to Prome with instructions to destroy all native craft 10 miles beyond that town so that nothing useful would fall into the hands of the enemy. Lt Penman in *Rita* was sent even further up the river to reconnoitre, while *Doris* was sent downstream where an enemy patrol was encountered and engaged. Two of the enemy were wounded.

Patrolling and the destruction of native craft continued but the situation became increasingly confused. The army commando under Musgrave was withdrawn at this point but eventually Johnston made contact with the 17th Indian Division and was told to base his force on Alanmyo as Prome had now been evacuated. The division was then withdrawn from the river and replaced by 1st Burma Division, consisting of the 1st, 2nd and 13th Brigades, and Johnston was told to continue patrolling and to act as liaison between the 1st and 13th Brigades on the east bank and the 2nd Brigade on the west. But on 6 April withdrawal again became inevitable and the flotilla moved back to Minhla where a new acquisition, *Harry*, named after the force's sergeant major, was added to the flotilla's strength. *Harry* was a diesel-engined junk and proved to be a useful if unusual vessel.

As the withdrawal of the British forces continued, Force Viper, often harassed by the Japanese, continued to patrol the river well below the front line. At the same time boats were sent upstream to destroy all water transport that might prove to be of any use to the enemy. By 15 April Yenangyaung was in flames, and the oilfields and their installations all destroyed. Their destruction was followed on 19 April by the blowing up of the Chauk and Lanywa oilfields, and by 24 April the military situation had deteriorated so much that Force Viper was ordered to ferry the elements of the 1st Burma Division that were on the eastern bank across the river at Sammeikon, 12 miles below Myingyan. This accomplished, they were to leave the Irrawaddy and move up the Chindwin to Monywa, from where they were to start patrolling again.

Then orders faced Johnston with two major problems: the entrance to the Chindwin was too shallow for the flotilla's vessels, and Force Viper possessed nothing remotely suitable for ferrying a large force of men. Penman was sent up the Chindwin to acquire what suitable craft he could for patrolling that river while Fayle was dispatched with the main part of the force to take the flotilla's stores to Myinmu some 30 miles up the Irrawaddy. Once there, he was

in shadow, and came across a small dump of ammunition which had been secreted there by the rest of Fayle's platoon. This enabled the three men to continue the fight until they virtually had command of the compound. But by 0430 hours they were again short of ammunition and they escaped undetected down to the river's edge and made their way back to the flotilla. For this extraordinary exploit Fayle was subsequently awarded the Military Cross, and Cpl Winters and Marine Shaw the Military Medal.

The battle at Padaung had reduced Force

to scuttle his vessels and transport the stores by bullock cart to Monywa on the Chindwin River. This left the problem of ferrying the troops of the 1st Burma Division, but this was luckily solved when three Irawaddy Flotilla Company boats, *Haingyi, Haifa* and *Waikata*, appeared. These were quite suitable for ferrying and they were promptly commandeered and taken to Sammeikon.

The ferrying operation began on 27 April, in the afternoon, and it was not completed until the early hours of 29 April. The marines worked without a break and in that time ferried across 320 bullock carts, mainly filled with stores, 640 bullocks and about 500 mules, as well as men, guns and vehicles. This achieved, Force Viper unloaded their boats of anything that might be of use and then sank them in mid-channel. They then joined Fayle and Penman at Monywa. Unfortunately, however, Penman had had no success in obtaining suitable craft as they were all employed shipping refugees upstream. He had applied to Army HQ for one craft to be released to Force Viper for patrolling but was told that none was available, but that the force would have to start patrolling as soon as a threat developed to Monywa. Faced with this 'Catch-22' situation it was decided to adopt a system of infiltration, and marines were put aboard two of the craft — which were stern-wheelers and unfamiliar to anyone in the force — to learn how they were handled.

On 1 May the town was attacked by the Japanese and Johnston and 18 of his force were soon embroiled in a fierce fire fight in an attempt to prevent the enemy crossing the river to enter the town. But eventually they were forced to withdraw and they made their way north to Alon where, the following morning, Johnston was ordered to organise and cover yet another ferrying operation, this time across the Chindwin at Shwegyn, some six miles below Kalewa. At Kalewa Johnston met up with the rest of Force Viper who had managed to escape upriver on a double-deck stern-wheeler, *Shillong*, which they were now working.

Lack of preparation made the ferrying at Shweign both time-consuming and difficult. Four double-deck and two single-deck stern-wheelers were used for the operation, and by 11 May the job was completed. The force then made its way up to Sittaung destroying any native craft it saw as it went. The enemy was now advancing rapidly and the general situation had deteriorated so markedly that there was now no question of being able to hold on to Burma, and the remnants of the army defending it now began its retreat to India. On 14 May the Chindwin Flotilla of Force Viper was moored across the river and sunk, and the main part of the force left with the army to march out to India, while Johnston, after one final mission, followed later with a smaller party.

Out of a total force of 107 only 48 managed to get out of Burma with the British forces but Force Viper had made its impression on the enemy for the Japanese had broadcast that if they caught any marines they would roast them and then cut them up into small pieces.

So ended one of the most courageous and curious operations ever carried out by the Royal Marines. 'As strange and gallant an amphibious expedition as any the Corps had ever been called upon to perform', was how an official account described it.

Below: Map of Irrawaddy and Chindwin rivers.

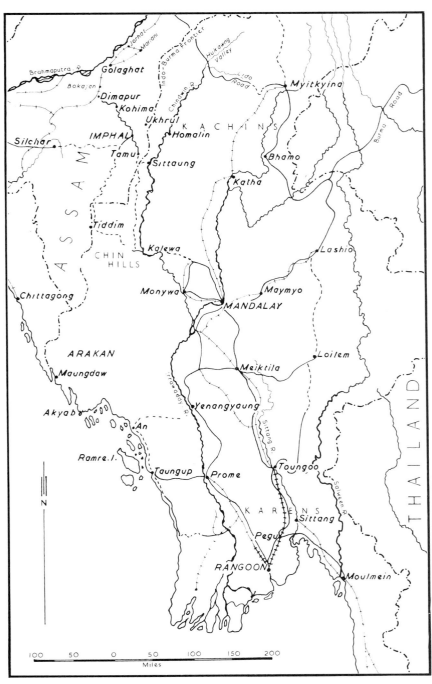

Guadalcanal

Destroyer firing support salvo.
USMC

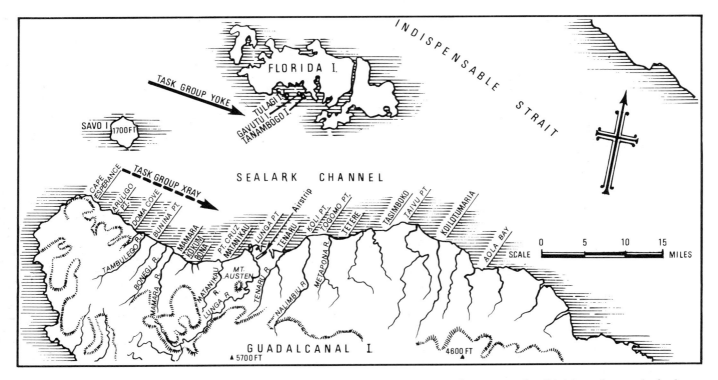

Above: Map of Guadalcanal and
Florida islands.
*Reproduced by kind permission of
Historical Branch, USMC*

*The Guadalcanal landings, on 7 August
1942, embraced several islands, but the main
marine force hit Guadalcanal Island, a rain-
soaked, jungle-choked, malaria-ridden slice
of land 90 miles long and 25 wide that was
part of the British Solomons, a scattered
group of islands some 750 miles east of the
southern tip of New Guinea.*

*For the US Marines Guadalcanal was the
first amphibious operation of World War 2.
This crucial first confrontation with the
hitherto totally victorious Japanese blooded
the marines and showed them that the enemy
was not invincible.*

*After it was over those who had fought in
the gruelling six-month campaign were able
to pass on the skills they had learnt to other
marines, and this was a critical factor in the
other island operations that followed.*

*Some have questioned the validity of the
landings, for the cost was high and the
strategic importance of Guadalcanal was not
overwhelming. But as others have pointed out
the Americans had to start somewhere. The
landings undoubtedly saved the southern
coast of New Guinea from invasion and
checked the Japanese advance to Australia
and New Zealand. After Guadalcanal the
Japanese never advanced again. It was the
turning point of the Pacific war, and that is
its significance.*

*What follows describes how Guadalcanal
was secured by the 1st Marine Division.
Others followed after the division was withdrawn on 9 December 1942 — the 2nd
Marine Division among them — and it was
these units which finally drove the Japanese
from the island. But it was 'The Old Breed',*
*the veteran 1st Division, that took the brunt
of the fighting and made victory possible.*

The landing force for Guadalcanal consisted
of 19,000 men of the 1st Marine Division
commanded by Maj Gen A. A. Vandegrift, a
veteran of several prewar campaigns. The
division was made up of the 1st and 5th
Marine Regiments of the 1st Division
(abbreviated to 1/1 and 5/1 respectively), the
2nd Marine Regiment of the 2nd Division
(2/2), the 1st Marine Raider Battalion, the
1st Parachute Battalion, and the 3rd Defense
Battalion. The troopships transporting the
force were escorted by a powerful fleet and
the combined force was under the command
of Rear-Adm Turner, a command structure
which was to cause problems and which later
enabled the US Marine Corps to establish
that, in future, the overall command of an
amphibious operation should be in the hands
of the marines.

When the possibility of landing on
Guadalcanal had been first discussed,
Vandegrift had expected that he would be
given several months to train his division in
New Zealand, the point of departure for the
invasion fleet. But it was then discovered that
the Japanese were building an airstrip on
Guadalcanal Island, making it essential that
the invasion be brought forward. As a consequence of this the division's rear echelon
only just had time to unload in New Zealand
and reload into the invasion ships before the
fleet sailed. After a poor rehearsal in Fiji the
landings took place on the morning of
7 August 1942.

The plan called for the division to be split

Left: Men of the 5th Marines coming ashore against scattered opposition. *USMC*

Below: A two-man emplacement in the Tenaru area. The marine on the left is holding a Browning automatic rifle, the other a Springfield. *USMC*

Bottom: This Navy PBY-5A plane was the first to land on Henderson Field, 12 August, shortly after it was completed by US engineers. It evacuated two wounded marines. *USMC*

into two task forces, Yoke and X-Ray, with five simultaneous landings: 1/1 and 5/1 (less 2nd Battalion), under Vandegrift, would land on Guadalcanal Island's north coast in the vicinity of the airstrip; Brig-Gen Rupertus, the Assistant Divisional Commander and in overall charge of the operation on the north side of Sealark Channel, would land on Florida Island — it proved to be unoccupied — with 1st Battalion 2/2; the 1st Raider Battalion, under Lt-Col 'Red Mike' Edson, with 2nd Battalion 5/1 in support, would land on Tulagi Island; and the Parachute Battalion, led by Maj Roberts, would tackle the smaller islands of Gavutu and Tanambogo which were linked by a causeway.

The landings, both to the north and south of Sealark Channel, took the Japanese completely by surprise, a combination of bad weather and poor Japanese communications enabling most of the force to land without opposition. The 1st and 3rd Battalions of 5/1 did come under attack soon after they came ashore east of the Tenaru River, but by the next afternoon, after meeting only scattered opposition, the 1st Battalion 1/1 occupied the airstrip and 1st Battalion 5/1 took over the deserted enemy strongpoint at Kukum on Lunga Pt. It was not until a patrol, penetrating further to the west, ran into strong opposition, that it was established that the enemy were on the island in strength and were prepared to fight to keep it.

On the north side of Sealark Channel the 1st Battalion 2/2 made two unopposed landings on Florida Island. On Tulagi, where a seaplane base was being established by the Japanese, a number of aircraft were

destroyed before they could get airborne and
the Raider Battalion landed without opposition. Later, however, thet met fierce
resistance when they came to a shovel-
shaped steep-sided ravine. Edson said:
'The walls of the ravine surrounded a flat
space which the British had used as a cricket
field and the Japs had dug innumerable large
caves into the limestone walls of the ravine,
and from the narrow mouths of these
dugouts they fired rifles, automatic rifles, and
machine guns. At 1030 that night they
attacked. They broke through between C and
A Companies, and C Company was
temporarily cut off. The Japs worked their
way along the ridge, and came to within 50
to 75 yards of my command post. The Nips
were using hand grenades, rifles and machine
guns. We suffered quite a few casualties, as
our men fought hard to hold the Japs back.
One machine gun company lost 50% of its
NCOs.'

During this fierce fighting the battalion's
mortarmen performed invaluable work
underlining the value of this weapon as a
piece of doggerel, published in the Division's
history, points out:

'We have a weapon nobody loves.
They say that our gun's a disgrace.
You crank up 200, and 200 more,
And it lands in the very same place.
Oh, there's many a gunner who's blowing his
top,
Observers are all going mad,
But our affection has lasted
For this old pig iron Bastard,
It's the best gun this world ever had.'

The next day the raiders counter-attacked
and began clearing the caves with TNT, the
only way to get at the enemy effectively. 'The
Nip defence', Edson said, 'was apparently
built around small groups in dugouts with no
hope of escape. They would stay in there as
long as there was one live Jap. There was a
radio for communication in nearly every one
of these holes'. The Japanese did, indeed,
resist to the last man but by late afternoon,
with the raiders being aided by elements of
the 2nd Battalion 5/1, the island was in the
hands of the marines. Mopping up went on
for days, but this swift victory brought Edson
the Navy Cross.

The Japanese also fought tenaciously on
the other two islands to the north of Sealark
Channel. A naval and air bombardment that
preceded the landings there had been
expected to neutralise their defences but they
had hidden themselves in coral caves and
well-constructed dugouts which protected
them from the worst of the bombardment. As
a consequence, units of 2/2 failed to gain a

34

Above left: This carrier torpedo plane joined MAG-23 in strikes against the Japanese. *USMC*

Left: One of the M3 light tanks which were used very effectively against the Japanese during the closing stages of the battle of the Tenaru. One of the earliest versions of the vehicle with the two sponson-mounted .30in machine guns which were deleted on later types. *USMC*

Bottom left: A 75mm pack howitzer in action from a captured Japanese emplacement. *USMC*

Above: Marine using captured Japanese flamethrower to blast enemy position. *USMC*

foothold at all on Tanambogo, while the Parachute Battalion, which landed on Gavutu, met murderous fire on the beaches. Within two hours they had been literally decimated, and though they managed to push inland and then south-east, while 2/5 headed for the other tip of the island, progress was painfully slow. As on Tulagi, the enemy had to be dislodged from their caves with TNT. One of the major exponents of this novel type of warfare was Capt Torgerson who, in the course of this short, sharp, bloody campaign, blasted more than 50 Japanese caves with his home-made bombs. An eye-witness wrote (in *Guadalcanal Diary* by Richard Tregaskis): 'His method was to tie 30 sticks of dynamite together, run to the cave mouth while four of his men covered it with rifles and sub-machine guns, light the fuse, shove the TNT in amongst the Japs, and run like hell. In his day's work Capt Torgerson used 20 cases of dynamite and all the available matches. His wristwatch strap had been broken by a bullet which creased his wrist. Another grazing bullet had struck his rear end. But that did not stop his pyrotechnic campaign.'

The Japanese fought so stubbornly on the island that some of them went to the extreme of hiding their weapons in the day and taking to the water to hide, returning at night to snipe at the marines. But by the Sunday evening (10 August) the paratroopers, with the help of reinforcements from 3rd Battalion 2/2, had cleared Tanambogo, with only a handful of Japanese escaping to Florida Island. They left behind nearly 1,500 dead. Marine casualties amounted to 108 dead and 140 wounded.

During this time the aircraft carriers giving the two task forces vital air cover were withdrawn. Too precious at this point in the war

to risk exposing them to the enemy, their commander, Rear-Adm Fletcher, ordered them from the area even earlier than he had warned he would during the planning stages of the landings. His caution was understandable, but it left the marines — and the ships still unloading their supplies — badly exposed, as it did the surface forces remaining in the area; and it enabled the Japanese Eighth Fleet, dispatched by the Japanese High Command when it heard of the landings, to enter Sealark Channel unopposed. As a result they sank three American cruisers and damaged another, and sank the Australian cruiser, HMAS *Canberra*.

The battle of Savo Island — as this encounter came to be called — was a stunning defeat for the Americans, but it did not cripple the invasion of Guadalcanal because the Japanese did not press home their advantage and destroy the helpless transports still unloading supplies off Lunga Pt for the five marine battalions now on Guadalcanal Island. But with their air support gone and their naval support badly mauled it was essential that the marines should hold Henderson Field — as the airstrip was now called, after a marine aviation hero of Midway — and a defensive ring was thrown around it. To prevent the Japanese landing troops within this perimeter, Vandegrift ordered a defensive front facing seaward to be constructed from Kukum eastward around Lunga Pt to the mouth of the Ilu River. He then gave the highest priority to completing the airstrip so that air support could be flown in.

These were critical days for the marines. They were constantly harassed both from the air and from the sea, and their foothold on the island, only some seven miles long, was

only insecurely defended by hurriedly dug lines. Though short of food and essential supplies, the marines managed to hold this line against an enemy still surprised and disorganised by the landings, until the airstrip was completed. But it soon became obvious to the marines that the landings had been badly planned and hurriedly executed. If the Japanese had been over-extended in their conquest of the Pacific, the Americans had, perhaps, been over-hasty in trying to exploit that weakness. To the men involved the landing quickly became known as 'Operation Shoestring'.

Help was at hand, however, and on 20 August, 31 aircraft, the forward echelon of Marine Air Group 23, arrived at Henderson Field. These were soon followed by naval and army air units, and this motley collection of brave flyers became known as the 'Cactus Air Force'; 'Cactus' being the code name for the landings on Guadalcanal Island. They were commanded by a legendary marine officer, Brig-Gen Geiger, who arrived on the island on 3 September.

Before the arrival of this air support, on 18 August, the marines struck against a heavy concentration of Japanese located by earlier patrols on the far side of the Matanikau River which flowed seven miles to the west of Lunga Pt. The plan was to capture the village of Matanikau with a seaborne landing at Kokumbona to the west and a two-pronged advance by land, one from inland, and the other along the shore. The attack seemed to be successful, but throughout the coming months this area proved the toughest for the marines to clear. With the freedom to move at will outside the marines' perimeter, the Japanese could concentrate their forces, and disperse them, at will, and the thick jungle was perfect cover for such tactics.

On the same day as the marines began operating to the west of their perimeter the Japanese landed 900 troops, part of a force under the command of Col Ichiki, at Taivu, to the east of the perimeter. They began moving against Henderson Field and soon fierce fighting developed on the banks of the Ilu River (Alligator Creek), the mouth of which was partially blocked by a sandbar. The Japanese stormed across this sandbar for frontal assault on the marines' line, and they also tried to outflank the defenders by swimming round behind their lines. Some broke through the wall of fire and desperate hand-to-hand fighting ensued. Cpl Wilson's automatic rifle jammed just as three Japanese attacked him in his foxhole, Wilson grabbed a machete and disposed of the first one who rushed at him. He then leapt out of his foxhole, rushed the other two before they could fire, and killed them both with the

Above: Moving inland after the landings. *USMC*

Left: A wireless operator reports back on enemy positions soon after landing. *USMC*

Below: This was the first gun in action after the Guadalcanal landings. In four hours it had been transferred from ship to shore, emplaced and was firing. Its initial salvo knocked out an enemy AA position. *USMC*

machete. Another corporal, John Shea, found himself in an equally desperate situation when his gun also jammed. As he dived for a foxhole to give himself cover while he cleared it, a Japanese, who was already in the foxhole, stabbed him in the left leg with a bayonet. Shea kicked the Japanese in the stomach, drove him against the wall of the foxhole and, managing to clear his gun, shot him.

A machine gun team, consisting of Pte Al Schmid, Pte John Rivers, and Cpl Leroy Diamond, were among the many marines who fought heroically in that first battle. When Rivers was shot while manning the gun, Schmid stepped over his body and took his place. They knocked out an enemy machine gun and killed several advancing Japanese, but first Diamond was wounded and then Schmid. Diamond was hit in the arm and Schmid was temporarily blinded by a grenade. When Schmid pulled out his 0.45in revolver, Diamond thought that as they were now completely surrounded, Schmid was going to shoot himself. 'Don't do that Smitty,' Diamond pleaded 'don't shoot yourself.' 'Hell,' Schmid replied. 'Don't you worry. I'm just going to wait and get the first Jap that comes in here.' 'But you can't see,' Diamond reasoned. 'I don't have to see,' Schmid retorted. 'You just tell me which way he's coming and I'll get him.' But the attack by then had faded and Diamond and Schmid survived, and were awarded the Navy Cross.

Pte Harding was one of many marines who had to fight for their lives in close combat with the enemy as James D. Holan and Gerald Frank later related in their book, *Out in the Boondocks:*

'Tracers were coming over like white bees and I thought any minute I'd get it. Then the bums started to throw flares behind us. The whole place was lit up like a church. Every time one blew up, I stuck my face right into the sand. Then I started crawling toward my hole again. I wanted to get in there badly. I was nearly there when a flare exploded behind me. I almost jumped out of my pants. In front, a little off to my left, a guy was making for my hole. I saw him clearly in that sudden white light. When it died out, I crawled forward again. I could see the dim form of this fellow crawling as I was. But I didn't know if he was marine or Jap. I got closer. Another flare went up. When that died out, I knew he was a Jap — and I'd have to fight him for that hole. The bastard was trying to use my foxhole. I laid down my '03 [Springfield 1903 rifle] and pushed it forward with my right hand, ready for action. I stalked him. He'd move forward. Then I would. Once I heard him yell in Japanese. I think he was yelling orders to someone behind me. I didn't wait to listen. I crawled

Above: Dragging dead Japanese from a captured light machine gun nest. *USMC*

Left: 80mm mortar section in action. *USMC*

Below: A patrol moving out. *USMC*

again. Suddenly my right hand jerked. It stung like hell. I must have been nicked. I put my hand to my mouth. It was wet and salty. I kept crawling. Now another flare banged off. The Jap halted. When the flare died away, I crawled around one side of the hole. I knew he went around the other. I waited, holding my rifle tight as hell. First I saw his hand, then his arm, then his head. He was coming closer inch by inch. I was afraid to fire because the muzzle blast would give me away. Now I saw him clearly. His head was down, almost touching his wrist, like a dog hit by a car, and he was crawling. He was about a foot from me when I swung my rifle at him. I felt my bayonet slash his arms and he let out a yell. I didn't give him a chance to pull anything. I jumped and landed on his back. I got his neck in the crook of my right arm and squeezed. His head was buried in my chest. He began to gurgle. I tightened on him with all my might. He began to kick as he fought to get loose. He kicked so hard one foot kicked me in the back. It was a terrific blow, and I almost let go. I began to get a little panicky. I was afraid I'd suddenly go weak and he'd twist out. I kept thinking, I'll get it now, I'll get it now, I'll get it now. It ran through my head like a merry-go-round. The damn tracers were buzzing by, and every

Above left: A machine gunner leading a patrol across a jungle stream. *USMC*

Left: Though under fire from snipers these men of 5th Marines calmly carry a wounded buddy to safety. *USMC*

Top: Carefully checking a captured enemy bivouac area. *USMC*

Above: A captured Japanese field piece. *USMC*

once in a while a mortar would blow up right close. I don't know why I wasn't killed because I must have been a clear target. But the Jap was getting weaker. Finally he stopped twisting. I held on for a minute. You can't trust a Jap. Then I let go. He was limp. I lay there breathing hard. He didn't move. I pushed him with my leg. He was dead.'

At 0300 hours, with the issue still in doubt, the Regimental Commander, Col Cates, called down an artillery concentration, and this caught the Japanese in the open and caused heavy casualties. One battalion commander, Lt-Col Pollock, said:
'From about 4am to daylight the battle continued more or less as a state of siege, with all weapons firing and no one knowing the exact situation. When daylight came, the gruesome sight on the sandspit became visible. Dead Japs were piled in rows and on top of each other from our gun positions outward. Some were only wounded and continued to fire after playing dead. Others had taken refuge under a two-foot sand embankment and around trunks of the coconut trees, not fifty yards from our lines.'

Slowed down by well laid wire and by the accurate fire of the marines, Ichiki's men

were eventually stopped and then routed, first by the artillery concentration, then by the 1st Battalion 1/1, under Lt-Col Cresswell, which outflanked them and took them in the rear, then by the marine fighters of Marine Fighter Squadron VMF 223 strafing them, and by light tanks.

When the battle of the Tenaru, as it was called through mistakenly calling the Ilu River the Tenaru, eventually petered out, nearly 800 Japanese bodies littered the ground, and later the balance of Ichiki's landing force was turned back by marine aircraft before it had a chance to land. Ichiki committed suicide. However, other landings were soon made by the Japanese and the Americans had neither the strength in the air or at sea to prevent them. But they did make them hazardous operations and the Japanese soon took to using fast transport destroyers in order to evade the American warships and land their troops as quickly as possible. This means of transportation soon became known to the marines as the 'Tokyo Night Express'. One such landing that deposited a strong Japanese force near Tasimboko was attacked by elements of the Raider and Parachute Battalions which, with 2nd Battalion 5/1, had been moved across Sealark Channel to reinforce Guadalcanal Island. The raiders attacked the enemy from the sea on 18 September. They captured a mass of supplies but most of the landing force evaded them by fleeing inland. Later, however, when contact was made with the Japanese they put up fierce opposition with heavy 75mm artillery fire. The crews of these guns, defended by riflemen and machine gunners, had to be picked off one by one, a desperately hazardous undertaking. Pte Klejnot, however, disposed of one of the crew by himself. 'I picked off one, and the other went and hid behind some boxes in a little ammunition dump. I fired into the dump and set it afire.' Eventually the Japanese force slipped away into the jungle and the marines returned to their perimeter, but within a few days the force had regrouped to the south and then launched a well organised assault against the marines' lines.

The marines' perimeter was not a continuous line of defence — Vandegrift did not have enough men for this — but a series of defensive positions which took what advantage they could of the terrain. All units were deployed around it, including pioneer, engineer and amphibious tractor battalions. Lt-Col Edson, who now had the Parachute Battalion under his command, had anticipated such an attack and had deployed his men below the southern trip of Lunga Ridge and had ordered them to dig in there.

The attack, when it came on the night of 12/13 September, was ferocious and

Top: Members of 2nd Battalion, 2nd Marines crossing a pontoon bridge over the Matanikau river. *USMC*

Above: Marines pose amongst a captured Japanese communication command post deep in the jungle near the Kokumbona river. *USMC*

got many a strike that night. Every time one of our grenades would explode, it would be followed by screams and wild shouts. It certainly was some night. Colonel Edson was in the middle of all this. He was wearing a regular helmet and fatigue dungarees. You couldn't tell him from any other marine. He directed the fight the whole night long, and he did a hell of a job, believe me. About dawn four Japs charged up the ridge. I could only see the upper part of their bodies because they were moving through high grass. One Jap had a Tojo flag; the other three monkeys were behind him with fixed bayonets. I spotted the shot for 200 yards. Our mortar shell landed square on the nose, and hit the Jap with the flag. All of them were wiped out. There was flying dirt — and no more flag, no more Japs.'

On 13 September the Cactus Air Force kept the Japanese at bay, but at 2100 hours that night the assaults were renewed with great ferocity. Two Japanese battalions — screaming 'Gas! Gas!' — threw themselves against the exhausted raiders who held on doggedly to the last remaining spur on the ridge. Japanese snipers infiltrated the marines' flanks and at one point Gen Vandegrift's Command Post was on the verge of being surrounded, three Japanese being killed right in front of him. But somehow the marines clung to those last few yards of vital ground. They knew that if that last spur was lost so, almost certainly, was Henderson Field which was dominated by the ridge.

The turning point of the battle — which also came to be called the Battle of Edson's Ridge or Bloody Ridge — came when the Parachute Battalion counter-attacked, and though it took 40% casualties, what remained of the Japanese force was eventually forced to withdraw. At dawn it was pursued by Cactus Air Force fighters, and two additional attacks on the perimeter to the east and west were also successfully driven off. The marines on Guadalcanal had survived their stiffest test yet.

Reinforcements in the form of 3rd Battalion 2/2 now arrived from across Sealark Channel and the 1st Division's 7th Marines were also dispatched from Samoa to join the rest of the division on Guadalcanal. This enabled the remnants of the Parachute Battalion to be withdrawn, the first troops to be evacuated from the island. These extra troops — and the fact that Gen Geiger's motley collection of flyers could guarantee a minimum of 60 operational aircraft — improved Gen Vandegrift's position appreciably. He could at last afford to increase his attacks on the enemy lurking in the jungle beyond his perimeter, and could also increase his perimeter.

supported by gunfire from a Japanese light cruiser and three destroyers in Sealark Channel. Hand-to-hand fighting developed, and the Raiders' right flank was isolated and broken. 1st Sgt Marasciullo led a mortar team during this crucial battle for Lunga Ridge which the marines later called 'Boot Hill' because so many of them died there with their boots on. Marasciullo said:

'The night it began the Japs sent over a smokescreen. It was like a fog seeping through our boondocks. It smelled like burning powder. A runner came up from our CO and went from platoon to platoon with the order: "Grab guns and ammunition. Move to the top of the ridge. Get going!" The Japs were in the gulley and we moved fast, so that we arrived there just in time to meet their drive up the hill. God it was dark that night. Machine guns started, mortars began bursting, and our own artillery shells were whistling about. Yet you could tell the difference between our machine guns and the Japs. We sang bass and the Japs sang soprano. Even the bullets were different. Their tracers had a brighter hue than ours. They were purple, white, and streaked the night like a rainbow. All night long we lay on the ridge and bowled hand grenades down the hill to the gulley. We

As a first move to take the initiative, Gen Vandegrift sent out the 7th Marines' 1st Battalion, commanded by Lt-Col 'Chesty' Puller, as a reconnaissance force to explore the enemy's strength inland and to the west of the Matanikau River. Puller's men were soon in contact with the enemy, a substantial force holding up their advance on the slopes of Mt Austen. But after returning his wounded under a two company escort, and being reinforced by 2nd Battalion 5/1, Puller pressed on westwards to the river and then northwards along its east bank where he again encountered strong opposition. Heavy enemy mortar and machine gun fire was coming from the ridges to the west of the river and from Matanikau itself, and it soon became obvious that the enemy was present in far greater strength than intelligence reports from air and ground patrols had indicated. A crossing of the river was attempted but failed and Gen Vandegrift then cancelled his plan for the Raider Battalion to move westwards to Kokumbona. Instead he ordered them to strike at the enemy's rear, and at his right flank, once the raiders had managed to cross the river. At the same time Puller would attack the Japanese by crossing the river further inland and then striking north.

It was soon found, however, that the enemy had forestalled this plan as they had themselves crossed the Matanikau in strength. Fierce fighting developed. A message from the raiders was misunderstood to mean that their attack had been successful and it was decided to land the men of Puller's battalion who had earlier returned with the battalion's wounded in the vicinity of Kokumbona to cut off the supposedly defeated enemy. This confusion had tragic consequences for though the marines landed unopposed they were soon attacked from the air and later their position was surrounded. Their communications were destroyed and the destroyer, assigned the task of giving them covering fire, temporarily neutralised when it had to take evasive action to escape the enemy's air attacks. The CO of the landing force was killed and there were many casualties before the marines managed to extricate themselves. The Raiders in the meantime were also receiving heavy casualties and were badly mauled before they were extricated.

This sharp reversal of fortunes showed that Vandegrift's forces were very far from being able to dominate the situation. Indeed, with the Japanese now shelling Henderson Field from their positions by the Matanikau River and establishing strong bridgeheads across it, the battle for the island again looked critical. Gen Vandegrift knew he had to dislodge the Japanese from their new positions, and that it must be done without delay. He therefore immediately dispatched

Below left: Map of first phase of the battle for Edson's Ridge, night of 12/13 September.
Reproduced by kind permission of Historical Branch, USMC

Below: Map of the final phase of the battle for Edson's Ridge, night of 13 September.
Reproduced by kind permission of Historical Branch, USMC

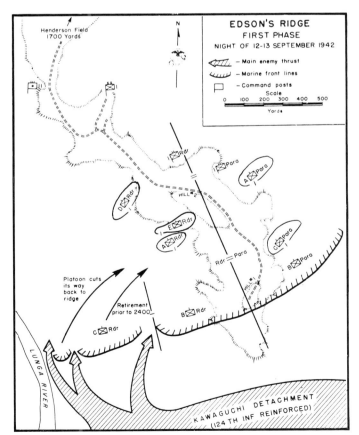

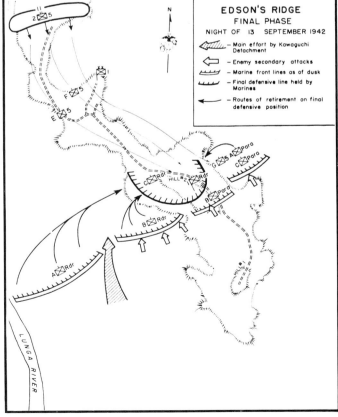

five marine battalions to trap and rout the Japanese in the area west of the perimeter before they could assemble in strength.

The 3rd Battalion 5/1, later reinforced by the raiders, threw back one enemy bridgehead near the coast after desperate hand-to-hand fighting, and inland 1st Battalion 7/1 under Puller inflicted heavy losses on a Japanese force which itself was about to attack the perimeter from the south. These successes threw the Japanese offensive off balance but it did not change the overall critical position of the marines who were coming under increasing pressure from an enemy determined to expel them. Guadalcanal Island had by now become a place where both the Americans and the Japanese had decided to stay and beat the enemy. It was a struggle of wills as well as of manpower and supplies. Neither side would yield, and, despite reinforcements in the form of two army units, the 164th Infantry and the American Division, Vandegrift's position

remained precarious as the enemy's naval forces and long range artillery kept up a heavy bombardment on Henderson Field.

On 13 October only 42 of the Cactus Air Force's 90 aircraft were operational, and the next day the 'Tokyo Night Express' landed an additional 3,000 Japanese troops. It looked as if the marines' foothold on the island was no longer tenable, for without sufficient air support there was little hope of holding off the greatly strengthened enemy for long. In addition, two months of fierce combat in extremely hostile terrain, combined with increasing attacks of malaria and other tropical diseases, was beginning to take its toll on the beleaguered force, and men and supplies were still not arriving in sufficient quantity. Many men of 2nd Battalion 7/1, for instance, had no socks, and the Under-Secretary for the Navy, James V. Forrestal, had told Adm Ghormley, the overall C-in-C, after he had visited Guadalcanal, that if the American people ever got to hear of the

Above: Marines preparing to move up to the line. The trucks are captured Japanese ones. *USMC*

Top right: Amphibious tractors moving down river to deliver ammunition to marine units engaged in a battle to the east. *USMC*

Centre right: Marines moving up to the fighting on the Matanikau river. *USMC*

Right: Dead Japanese after the bitter fighting on Edson's Ridge. *USMC*

shortages there would be a revolution. But Ghormley, because of America's European commitments, had been forced, against his better judgement, to strip his rear positions of fighting troops in order to reinforce Guadalcanal as best he could. In short the situation was grim. But the marines were not prepared to give in now and when on 21 October the Japanese launched their anticipated attack across the Matanikau at the perimeter the marines fought with great determination and drove the enemy back. Again the Japanese attacked and again they were driven back, a heavy artillery bombardment from 10 batteries of the 11th Marines virtually annihilating the attacking force.

However, while the marines were engaged in driving off the danger to their western perimeter another force of Japanese was assembling for an attack from the south, and on the morning of 24 October men from 3rd Battalion 7/1 observed that a strong enemy force had infiltrated during the night to their left rear and had outflanked them. The 2nd Battalion 7/1 were therefore sent forward to face this new threat but when the attack came it almost overwhelmed the battalion and only the most courageous fighting saved the marines from being completely overrun. At a critical moment in the battle Maj Conoley, the 2nd Battalion's executive officer, led a small force of 17 men composed of communications personnel, company runners, cooks, messmen and a few riflemen, and retook a position that had been overrun.

One position, however, the Japanese did not overrun was the one held by Sgt Paige, and his bravery during this battle won him a battlefield commission and a Medal of Honor. In his history of the First Marine Division, *The Old Breed*, George McMillan quotes Paige's description of how he and his platoon drove off an attack on the night of 25/26 October:

'All of us must have seen the Japs at the same time. Grenades exploded everywhere on the ridge-nose, followed by shrieks and yells. It would have been death to fire the guns because muzzle flashes would have given away our positions and we could have been smothered and blasted by a hail of grenades. Stansbury, who was lying in the foxhole next to mine was pulling out grenade-pins with his teeth and rolling the grenades down the side of the nose. Leipart, the smallest guy in the platoon, and my particular boy, was in his foxhole delivering grenades like a star pitcher. Then I gave the word to fire. Machine guns and rifles let go and the whole line seemed to light up. Pettyjohn yelled down to me that his gun was out of action. In the light from the firing I could see several Japs a few feet away from Leipart. Apparently he had been hit because he was down on one knee. I knocked off two Japs with a rifle but a third drove his bayonet into Leipart. Leipart was dead: seconds later so was the Jap. After a few minutes, I wouldn't swear to how long it was, the blitz became a hand-to-hand battle. Gaston was having trouble with a Jap officer, I remember that much. Although his leg was nearly hacked off and his rifle all cut up, Gaston finally connected his boot with the Jap's chin. The result was one slopehead with one broken neck.

'Firing died down a little, so evidently the first wave was a flop. I crawled over to Pettyjohn, and while he and Faust covered me I worked to remove a ruptured cartridge and change the belt feed pawl. Just as I was getting ready to feed in a belt of ammo, I felt something hot on my hand and a sharp vibration. Some damned slopehead with a light machine gun had fired a full burst into the feeding mechanism and wrecked the gun.

'Things got pretty bad on the second wave. The Japs penetrated our left flank, carried away all opposition and were possibly in a position to attack our ridge-nose from the rear. On the left, however, Grant, Payne and Hinson stood by. In the center, Lock,

Swanek, and McNabb got it and were carried to the rear by corpsmen. The Navy boys did a wonderful job and patched up all the casualties, but they were still bleeding like hell and you couldn't tell what was wrong with them so I sent them back. That meant all my men were casualties and I was on my own.'

Paige then gathered more riflemen and another machine gun and in the half light of dawn continued the fight. He would fire his machine gun and then shift his position before a rain of grenades fell where he'd just been. He then led the riflemen in a charge down from his position, routing what remained of the enemy. For three days Paige and his men remained in position before being withdrawn. 'On the third day,' Paige said, 'we marched twelve miles back to the airport. I never knew what day it was, and what's more I didn't care.'

Further to the east of Sgt Paige's position and directly south of the airstrip an enemy force not previously known to the marines now struck at the perimeter. At dawn on 25 October and again that night the Japanese assaulted the positions of 1st Battalion 7/1.

Below: A Raider Battalion, led by a native scout, move out on patrol. *USMC*

Right: Flamethrowers were effective weapons with which to flush out the enemy. Here two marines can be seen advancing cautiously with their flame throwers ready for use. *USMC*

Below right: Not many prisoners were taken on Guadalcanal but when they were they were usually ready to talk. Here two intelligence officers question a Japanese. *USMC*

Screaming and yelling they attacked at a point known to the marines as Coffin Corner, but, with the help of 2nd Battalion 164th Infantry, Puller's men held their line. One company ran out of ammunition and was told by Puller to hold with the bayonet. It did.

But Sgt Basilone of C Company did not run out of ammunition and he used his machine gun to such good effect that in the recommendation for his Medal of Honor, the first to be awarded to an enlisted marine, Puller said he had 'contributed materially to the defeat and virtually the annihilation of a Japanese regiment.' Basilone said in an interview with Marine Combat Correspondent Diggery Venn:

'When the first wave came at us the ground just rattled. We kept firing and drove them back, but our ammunition was getting low, so I left the guns and started running to the next outfit to get some more. Soon after I got back, a runner came in and told me that at the emplacements on the right Japs had broken through. With their knives they had killed two of the crew and wounded three, and the guns were jammed. I took off up the trail to see what had happened. I found Evans there. He had his rifle by him, and was screaming at the Japs to come on. What a guy he is! He's only 18-years-old and runs around barefoot all the time.

'After that I came back to my own guns, grabbed one of them and told the crew to follow me. Up the trail we went. I was carrying the machine gun by the tripod. We left six dead Japs on the trail. While I fixed the jams on the other two guns up there, we started to set up. We were really pinned down. Bullets were smacking in to the sandbags.

'The Japs were still coming at us, and I rolled over from one gun to the other, firing them as fast as they could be loaded. The ammunition belts were in awful shape as they had been dragged on the ground. I had to scrape mud out of the receiver.

'They kept coming and we kept firing. We all thought our end had come. Some Japs would sneak through the lines and get behind us. It got pretty bad because I'd have to stop firing every once in a while, and shoot behind me with my pistol. At dawn, our guns were burnt out. Altogether we got rid of 26,000 rounds.

'After that I discovered I was hungry, so I went to the CP (Command Post) to see about getting chow. All we could get was crackers and jam.'

The fighting continued with unremitting fierceness throughout the night and 3rd Battalion 164th Infantry had to be thrown into the battle. But by dawn the back of the Japanese attack had been broken and —

despite renewed assaults the following night — Henderson Field was once again safe from immediate attack and Puller had earned his third Navy Cross.

With the failure of these attacks, the best co-ordinated yet to throw the Americans off Guadalcanal Island, the Japanese offensive petered out for the time being. And just as they were at their height, on 24 October, thousands of miles to the east, decisions were being made that would finally turn the tide for the Americans on the Guadalcanal. For at last it was beginning to be realised in America that the 1st Marine Division was involved in a life-or-death struggle which, if successful, could spell the beginning of the end for the hitherto invincible Japanese forces and on that date President Roosevelt temporarily overrode America's agreement with her allies that the defeat of Germany was the first priority and personally ordered that the marines on Guadalcanal should receive every possible assistance. Two new American offensives were now put into operation. A second front had been advocated for some time by Adm Turner but was opposed by Gen Vandegrift. Against the latter's advice a force which included the Raiders, now commanded by Lt-Col Carlson, were landed at Aola Bay some 40 miles east of the Lunga River where a new American airstrip was planned. To the west, Vandegrift, determined to break the strength of the Japanese in the Matanikau area once

and for all, launched an attack across the Matanikau River on the night of 31 October with the 5th Marine Regiment, now commanded by Col Edson, with 2nd Marines in reserve. 1st Battalion 5/1 met stiff resistance when they encountered the enemy at the base of Pt Cruz. The battle lasted three days before the enemy were virtually wiped out.

As Edson was fighting to clear the Matanikau area west of the perimeter the now battle-worn 2nd Battalion 7/1, which had fought so bravely the previous month, was involved in yet another confrontation with a Japanese force which had been landed to the east of the Metapona River and in the area of Koli Pt. After a forced march to the area, contact was made with the enemy. But the battalion then suffered the severe handicap of losing all communication with divisional HQ so that air and artillery support could not be called for. Consequently they were forced to withdraw across the Metapona River to prevent an attack developing from their rear. Once on the west bank of the river they were able to re-establish contact with Divisional HQ and were at once reinforced by Puller's battalion which was brought in by boat. A counter-attack was then mounted with two battalions of 164th Infantry attacking from the south, and with Carlson's Raiders which were ordered west from Aola Bay as it was now accepted that Adm Turner's second front was no longer a practicable proposition.

Below: Patrolling up the Tenaru river. Note the native guide. *USMC*

Right: Map of Carlson's Raiders' historic patrol, 4 November-4 December. *Reproduced by kind permission of Historical Branch, USMC*

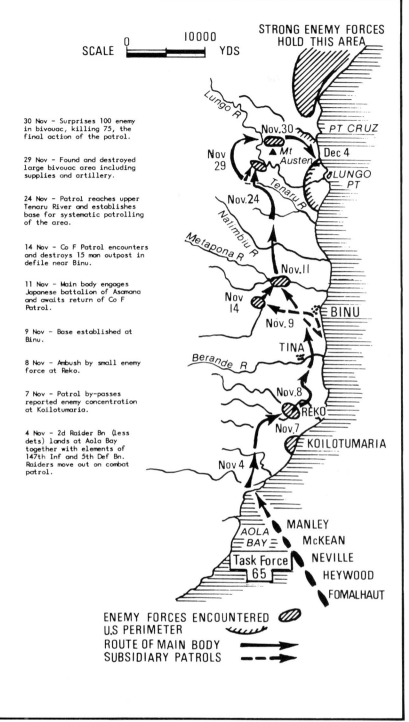

SCALE 0 ——10000—— YDS

STRONG ENEMY FORCES
HOLD THIS AREA

30 Nov - Surprises 100 enemy in bivouac, killing 75, the final action of the patrol.

29 Nov - Found and destroyed large bivouac area including supplies and artillery.

24 Nov - Patrol reaches upper Tenaru River and establishes base for systematic patrolling of the area.

14 Nov - Co F Patrol encounters and destroys 15 man outpost in defile near Binu.

11 Nov - Main body engages Japanese battalion of Asamona and awaits return of Co F Patrol.

9 Nov - Base established at Binu.

8 Nov - Ambush by small enemy force at Reko.

7 Nov - Patrol by-passes reported enemy concentration at Koilotumaria.

4 Nov - 2d Raider Bn (less dets) lands at Aola Bay together with elements of 147th Inf and 5th Def Bn. Raiders move out on combat patrol.

Lungo R.
Nov.30
Nov 29
Nov.24
Nov.11
Nov 14
Nov. 9
Nov.8
Nov.7
Nov 4
PT CRUZ
Mt Austen
Dec 4
LUNGO PT
Tenaru R.
Nalimbiu R.
Metapona R.
BINU
TINA
Berande R.
REKO
KOILOTUMARIA
MANLEY
McKEAN
NEVILLE
HEYWOOD
FOMALHAUT
AOLA BAY
Task Force 65

ENEMY FORCES ENCOUNTERED
U.S PERIMETER
ROUTE OF MAIN BODY
SUBSIDIARY PATROLS

---

the jungle. They were then pursued by Carlson's Raiders who, in an extraordinary three-week campaign in which they marched 150 miles and fought a dozen running battles, killed nearly 500 Japanese. For this feat Carlson was awarded his third Navy Cross.

While this historic patrol was in progress the Japanese made their last all-out effort to dislodge the tenacious 1st Marine Division. The veteran Japanese 30th Division, 10,000 strong, was sent to Guadalcanal in a fleet of 11 transports protected and preceded by a powerful fleet of Japanese warships which was to neutralise the airstrips (a second near Henderson Field had been built) and support the landing.

But this task force clashed with the US Navy and though it sank two American cruisers and four destroyers the Japanese also suffered heavy losses and were prevented from neutralising the airstrips. This enabled the Cactus Air Force to continue operating which it did very successfully, sinking seven of the 11 transports before they got anywhere near the beaches. Then, at dawn on 15 November, the four remaining transports were run ashore in an attempt to get the troops on board onto the island. But the Cactus Air Force aircraft and the 5in batteries of the 3rd Defense Battalion at Lunga Pt soon reduced the ships to flaming hulks. Those who managed to get ashore did not live long enough to put up a fight.

The Japanese were now a spent force. They could no longer reinforce to any great extent the dwindling number of troops they had on the island, and the decision was made to withdraw what remained of them. This was skilfully done while under heavy pressure from the large American forces that had been built up on the island and by the end of the first week of February 1943 there were no Japanese left to fight on Guadalcanal.

But before then — on 9 December 1942 — Gen Vandegrift handed over command to the US Army, and on his return to America he was personally decorated by President Roosevelt with the Medal of Honor. The exhausted 1st Marine Division was withdrawn at that time. For four bitter months they had fought a determined and skilled enemy in some of the worst terrain in the world. It had taken the brunt of the enemy's attacks and had started the irreversible decline of Japanese military power which was to be finally crushed with the atom bombs of Hiroshima and Nagasaki.

In the Pacific War the marines would fight other, even tougher, campaigns, and there were others which would be more famous. But Guadalcanal will always be remembered as the turning point. From then on it was only a matter of time.

The new Japanese landing force was now surrounded on three sides and on 8 November contact was made with it at Gavago Creek, a mile or so to the east of the Metapona River. In the fierce fighting that developed Puller was wounded and his battalion suffered 25% casualties which included half the battalion's officers. Hemmed in by army and marine units the enemy hit back hard for two days and then managed to evade the net by escaping through a gap in the lines, south along Gavago Creek and into

Tarawa

The importance of Tarawa in US Marine Corps history is that it was the corps' first opposed amphibious assault in pursuit of America's policy to clear the Pacific of the Japanese. In a series of island-hopping campaigns designed to by-pass some strongholds but to capture others the marines would carry the war right to the Emperor's doorstep.

Following this strategy, the capture of

Tarawa Atoll enabled the Americans to attack the next most northerly group of islands, the highly strategic Marshalls, which in turn meant that bringing Tokyo within range of American long-range bombers was one step nearer.

Gen Vandegrift put the importance of Tarawa in context when he commented that 'when the 2nd Marine Division landed on Betio Island, Tarawa Atoll on 20 November 1943, 20 years of Marine Corps study and work, already tested at Guadalcanal and at Bougainville, was put to an acid test.'

It was a test that the US Marine Corps survived, though only just. For, like Guadalcanal, but for different reasons, it was, at times, 'touch and go'. And the cost was high, higher than anyone thought possible or — many thought — right, and in his autobiography the corps commander at Tarawa, Lt-Gen Holland M. Smith, wrote that 'Tarawa should have been by-passed. Its capture — a mission executed by marines under direct orders from the high command — was a terrible waste of life and effort.' But Tarawa was a heroic battle, an epic, and the marines will always be remembered for it.

This picture: Amphibious tractors heading for shore. In the background can just be seen two warships of the support force. *USMC*

Below: The LVTs gave the first waves of marines some protection, but later waves had to wade ashore as the Higgins boats, seen here returning to their sister ship, could not cross the reef. The result was near-disaster. *USMC*

Tarawa Atoll consisted of a variety of small islands all of which needed to be cleared of the enemy along with other main island groups which made up the Gilbert Isles. Though there were clashes at these other groups, Makin and Apamama, it was on Betio, the largest island of Tarawa Atoll, that the main enemy force was located. Betio was heavily defended because the Japanese had built an airstrip on the island, a valuable prize that would enable the Americans to launch their attack on the Marshalls to the north.

Because Betio had such strong fortifications it was decided to reduce the enemy first by an overwhelming air and naval bombardment before sending the 2nd Marine Division, consisting of the 2nd, 6th and 8th Regiments (abbreviated 2/2, 6/2 and 8/2 respectively), ashore. 'We don't intend to neutralise the island,' said one briefing marine officer, 'we don't intend to destroy it, we will annihilate it.'

The 2nd Marine Regiment, plus 2nd Battalion 8/2, were to lead the assault in LVTs (Landing Vehicles Tracked) which would be able to negotiate a reef situated about 400yd

off the landing beaches. It had been deduced, rightly, that the Japanese were expecting any landing force to use the southern beaches not the northern ones because of this reef. Consequently the northern beaches were not mined to anywhere near the same extent as the southern ones. It was calculated, wrongly, that as the tide rose so the succeeding waves of assault troops would be able to pass over the reef in their LCMs (Landing Craft Mechanised) and LCVPs. It could be argued that in making this disastrous error the planners lost more lives than they ever saved by not landing on the southern side of the island.

On to this island, no larger than New York's Central Park, the Japanese had crammed what was estimated to be a force of between 2,500 and 2,700 highly trained Japanese naval troops, though this figure was later found to be an underestimate. The eventual total was nearer 4,000. The defences constructed for this force were intricate and extensive. A heavy log barrier sealed off the beaches from the land and there was a steep-sided tank trap running around the coastline covered by interlocking bands of fire from

Below: Marines taking cover behind the sea wall on Beach Red 3. *USMC*

numerous machine gun nests. These strongpoints were formidably built, some of the blockhouses having as much as five or six feet of coral sand on top of them, then a layer of logs, then more sand or coral blocks, yet more logs, all of which was supported by steel girders based on a solid concrete shelter or a roof of steel drums filled with concrete or coral. These emplacements varied in diameter between 15 and 45ft. Some were as much as seven feet high — the main Japanese command post was much higher — but many others were almost entirely buried in the coral rock. They seemed impervious to anything the marines could throw at them from the sea or air, and only a direct hit from either a 2,000lb bomb or a 16in shell had any visible effect on them. So each had to be destroyed individually, with flamethrowers, grenades and blocks of TNT. The enemy's resistance was fanatical and they were well armed and equipped, their weapons including the new 0.33in calibre rifle which had superseded the 6.5mm. Inside their fortifications they were well protected from blast, for each stronghold was divided into compartments so that every compartment had to receive a direct blast before the stronghold's occupants were completely silenced. Even the enemy's foxholes were divided up to maximise the security of the position, and were dug on a spider pattern with several trenches extending out from a single centre. There were also extensive anti-boat obstacles and mines, and these, with the help of the reef, were arranged to funnel any landing craft into prearranged fire lanes. The larger defensive weapons consisted of 8in coastal guns, AA and anti-boat guns, and light and heavy machine guns. In short Betio was a fortress.

The attack on the island began at dawn on 20 November 1943 with the USS *Colorado* and the USS *Maryland* replying to the fire from the Japanese coastal batteries, and it was followed by a naval and air bombardment of unparalleled ferocity. 'It's a wonder,' remarked one marine, as he watched Betio being pounded, 'that the whole goddam island doesn't fall apart and sink.' It seemed hard to believe that anything could be left alive when the barrage was raised for the marines to go ashore. Tragically, this optimism was quite ill-founded. To make matters worse various factors delayed the landing hour and this caused confusion which resulted in the assault group being without adequate support fire from either the sea or the air as they approached the beaches.

Although most of the larger defences like the coastal guns had been destroyed or neutralised by the air and naval bombardment the small pillboxes and strongpoints

had come through the hail of shells and bombs practically unscathed. And the lull in the bombardment before the marines landed had enabled the enemy to move troops to reinforce the northern beaches. The result was the marines were met with withering fire and though the first waves, carried in the LVTs, were relatively protected, the later waves were forced to disembark by the reef because the tide had not covered it sufficiently and wade the remaining distance to the beach under intense and accurate fire.

A quarter of an hour before the first assault troops landed a scout-sniper platoon led by 1-Lt Hawkins stormed the 550yd long pier that jutted out beyond the reef to prevent the Japanese on it enfilading the landing force. In fierce fighting he and his men, with the aid of flamethrowers, wiped out two Japanese machine gun nests on the pier and cleared it of the enemy. The platoon then went ashore ahead of the first assault wave and were instrumental during the next hours in silencing several enemy positions. Hawkins was hit on two separate occasions during these operations but continued to fight. He was eventually mortally wounded,

Below: Marines going over the sea wall. *USMC*

Bottom: Dragging back a badly wounded marine behind the shelter of the sea wall. *USMC*

Above: Col Shoup in conference at his Command Post. Shoup is holding the map case and is talking to Capt John J. Wade Jr. Just behind Wade with his hands on the butt of his pistol is Col Merritt A. Edson and to his left is Lt-Col Presley M. Rixey. Seated in front is Lt-Col Evan Carlson. *USMC*

Right: Attacking the bomb-proof shelter opposite the Burns Philp pier. *USMC*

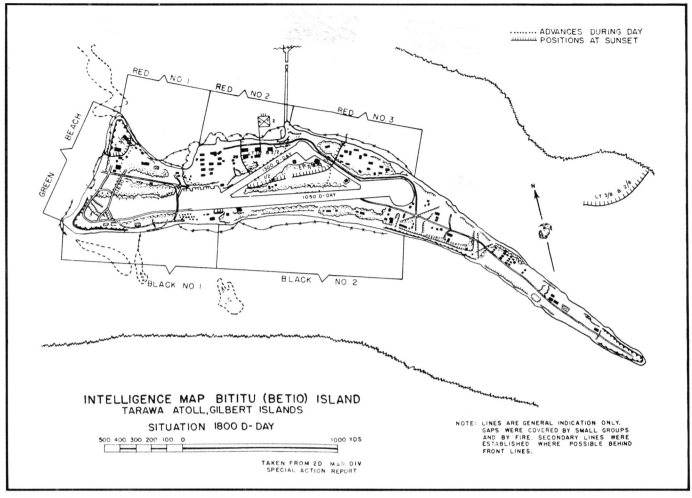

INTELLIGENCE MAP BITITU (BETIO) ISLAND
TARAWA ATOLL, GILBERT ISLANDS

SITUATION 1800 D-DAY

500 400 300 200 100 0   1000 YDS

TAKEN FROM 2D MAR DIV
SPECIAL ACTION REPORT

········· ADVANCES DURING DAY
ﬠﬠﬠﬠﬠ POSITIONS AT SUNSET

NOTE: LINES ARE GENERAL INDICATION ONLY.
GAPS WERE COVERED BY SMALL GROUPS
AND BY FIRE. SECONDARY LINES WERE
ESTABLISHED WHERE POSSIBLE BEHIND
FRONT LINES.

and was later posthumously awarded the Medal of Honor. 'It is not often that you can credit a first lieutenant with winning a battle,' the assault commander, Col Shoup, said when he heard of Hawkins' death, 'but Hawkins came as near to it as any man could. He was truly an inspiration.'

Supported by a company of tanks, the 2nd Marine Division hit Betio as follows: 2nd Battalion 8/2 (Maj Henry Crowe) landed on Red Beach 3 to the east of the pier; to Crowe's right 2nd Battalion 2/2 (Lt-Col Amey) landed on Red Beach 2; and on Amey's right 3rd Battalion 2/2 (Maj Schoettel) landed on Red Beach 1. The 1st Battalion 2/2 (Maj Kyle) was held back from the initial assault as reserve while the 6th Marines constituted the Corps reserve and was not, therefore, under the direct command of the divisional commander, Maj-Gen Julian C. Smith.

The first unit to hit the beaches was the 3rd Battalion 2/2. At 0910 hours the LVTs of this battalion left the water and moved up the coral sand of Red Beach under intense fire. On its left flank K Company was badly mauled when landing by a Japanese strong-point situated on the boundary between Red Beach 1 and Red Beach 2; and on its right

the enemy were able to bring to bear weapons placed to cover Green Beach on the western side of the island. Nevertheless, I Company on the right flank got ashore and began negotiating the log barrier and moving inland, but soon started receiving heavy casualties. The remainder of the battalion, including its Command Post, were in LCVPs and could not get over the reef. Relentless fire from the shore began to cut them down, and at 1000 hours Schoettel radioed Shoup: 'Receiving heavy fire all along beach. Unable to land all units. Issue in doubt.' Eight minutes later he radioed Shoup: 'Boats held up on reef of right flank Red 1. Troops receiving heavy fire in water.' Shoup radioed back that Schoettel should land the balance of his force on Red Beach 2 and they could then work their way west to join the rest of the battalion. Schoettel's reply was indicative of the seriousness of the situation. 'We have nothing left to land.'

To Schoettel's left Amey's men on Red Beach 2 were also in serious trouble. Having suffered heavily during the landing from heavy machine gun fire and anti-boat fire, enemy opposition on the battalion's right flank was so severe that it had great difficulty in gaining a foothold at all, while on the

Above: Map of Betio Island: the situation at 1800 on D-Day.
Reproduced by kind permission of Historical Section, USMC

This picture: A marine picking off a sniper. In the background to the right are some of the Japanese coastal defence guns. *USMC*

Below: The landing beaches. A wrecked LVT on Beach Red 2 lies askew against the sea wall. *USMC*

Above: Marines dash forward to capture enemy strongpoint which can be seen in the right background. *USMC*

eastern end of the beach F Company only landed after losing a great number of men. At 1000 hours they held a beachhead only 300yd wide and 75ft deep, and Amey, who had led them ashore with his pistol raised shouting, 'Come on, men, we're going to take the beach. Those bastards can't stop us,' was dead before he reached it. An observer, Lt-Col Jordan, now took command of the badly shaken battalion.

Only 2nd Battalion 8/2, commanded by Maj Crowe, which came ashore on Red Beach 3, landed with relatively few casualties. Two of their LVTs found a gap in the log barrier and pushed inland to the edge of the airstrip.

With the assault companies pinned down on the beaches it was now found that the waves coming in behind them could not get over the reef. Some of the marines in these waves managed to transfer to LVTs returning from the beaches but most had to wade through 500yd of waist deep water in full view of the enemy. It was a terrible ordeal and one well described by an Associated Press correspondent, William Hipple, who waded ashore with the marines. 'I hit the water waist-deep; cut off my Mae West life jacket with a knife. I couldn't unbuckle it. I followed the Colonel and the men splashing ahead. We were caught in a

crossfire from the right and left — machine guns, rifles and occasionally heavy-caliber automatic weapons. The bullets hissed on the water alongside all of us. As the water was now shallower, most of us got down on our hands and knees. We made spurts upright. My head was knocked back slightly. I felt the top of my steel helmet and it was red hot where a bullet had creased it. I dived completely under water, as I did many times afterwards, and tried to swim submerged as far as possible.'

Just before 1000 hours Kyle's battalion (1st Battalion 2/2) was ordered to land on Red Beach 2 and work its way west to aid the badly hit 3rd Battalion still pinned down and isolated on the western end of Red Beach 1, and at 1018 hours Gen Smith ordered part of the divisional reserve, 3rd Battalion 8/2 (Maj Ruud), ashore. They were ordered by Shoup to land on Red Beach 3 to help consolidate the small gains made by the regiment's 2nd Battalion. Both units had to wade ashore and Ruud's men were particularly badly hit, the battalion losing many of its officers and NCOs before even gaining the beach. Eventually, however, the survivors took up positions on the eastern perimeter with Crowe's battalion, and later they made small gains before being halted on the left flank by a massive strongpoint near a short wharf used in peacetime by the Burns-Philp trading company. At 1036 hours Gen Smith radioed the Vth Amphibious Corps: 'Successful landing on Beaches Red 2 and 3. Toe hold on Red Beach 1. Am committing one LT (landing team=battalion) from division reserve. Still encountering strong resistance throughout.'

All the assault troops were now ashore but the landing had taken a heavy toll. Marine WO John F. Leopold described the terrible scene of carnage after talking to a marine on the pier.

'He pointed to a marine lying on the pier and asked "Do you know who that is?" I said I didn't. I couldn't see. "It's the lieutenant," he said. "He's dead. The lieutenant was my best friend." That's the way it was. Everyone's best friend was lying dead. Sprawled on the beach, stiffened in the water, rocking with the tide as in a cradle. As far as you could see, men floated in the terrible stiffness of death. One marine was caught in barbed wire the Japanese had strung 600yd out into the water. He swayed back and forth slowly. When the tide went out the others went with it; he stayed right there. When the first plane landed four days later, the pilot said he saw dead men floating six or ten miles out to sea. He thought they were Japanese. They weren't. They were marines. They were our best men. They went in there with all they had, in and in, and those that came through took the island.'

Five sections of artillery of 1st Battalion 10/2 (Lt-Col Rixey) managed to get ashore during the day and were operational by dawn the following morning. The supporting tanks were also ashore very quickly, 10 M4 medium (Sherman) tanks as well as some light tanks landing in the fifth wave. Only two survived the landing on Red Beach 1 and both were later knocked out, though one continued to serve a useful purpose as flank protection during the first night as its bow machine gun was still operative. On Red Beach 3 all the tanks got ashore but by nightfall only one remained in action. The tanks designated for Red Beach 2 landed on Red Beach 3 but worked their way west where they proved invaluable in supporting the marines advancing towards the airstrip. Only one tank was lost.

Despite this tank support by midafternoon the general situation was still critical and Shoup and air reconnaissance patrols reported the vast majority of the landing force was still pinned down on all three beaches. On board the command ship, USS *Maryland*, Gen Julian Smith requested that the corps reserve (the 6th Regiment) be released to his control as he had only one

Above: One marine is poised to rush forward immediately the grenade his buddy is throwing has exploded. Fighting in small groups like this won Tarawa for the marines. *USMC*

landing team under his command left to commit, 1st Battalion 8/2, commanded by Maj Hays Jr. If the release of 6th Regiment was not granted he planned on leading the specialist troops under his command — engineers, artillerymen, pioneers, etc, whom he'd already organised into provisional battalions — on to the landing beaches. But the corps reserve was released and at 1625 hours Gen Smith ordered Hays' battalion, the last of his divisional reserve, ashore. However, communications throughout the day had been extremely poor and Hays never received the order, and consequently the battalion did not land on Red Beach 2 until the next morning.

The Japanese, too, were having serious problems with their communications, which had been completely disrupted by the massive bombardment, and it was for this reason that they did not manage to organise a concerted counter-attack on the frail, fragmented beachhead that first night. They did not get another chance.

Col Shoup, who had landed at 1100 hours, directed operations first from under the pier waist-deep in water and then set up his Command Post against a supposedly abandoned air raid shelter on Red Beach 2. (Supposedly, because the next morning it was discovered that the shelter contained a

number of Japanese so sentries were placed
at its entrance while Shoup got on with the
business of capturing Betio.) He knew the
next morning that if he was not to be driven
off the island that night he must at all costs
press forward and attack and divide the
Japanese garrison before they could muster
the counter-attack they should have launched
the night before. He therefore ordered Hays'
newly landed 1st Battalion 8/2 to strike west
and link up with Schoettel's cut-off 3rd
Battalion 2/2, and for the 1st and 2nd Battalion of the Division's 2nd Regiment to attack
south and seize the south coast of Betio.
Hays' men, however, had met even worse fire
than the marines on the previous morning,
and were decimated. Those that did manage
to struggle ashore arrived without
flamethrowers or demolitions, and could not
advance.

For the battalions striking south the
struggle to move inland was equally intense,
and could only be accomplished at all after a
few brave men had gone forward to destroy
enemy strongpoints with flamethrowers,
grenades and blocks of TNT tied together. 'If
these attempts were successful,' commented
one writer in a USMC monograph on
Tarawa, 'ie, if the marines attacking the positions lived long enough to complete their
task, then sometimes a whole platoon would
be able to move forward a few feet.' *Time*
correspondent Robert Sherrod described one
such encounter graphically.

'A marine jumped over the seawall and
began throwing blocks of fused TNT into a
coconut-log pillbox about 15 feet back of the
seawall against which we sat. Two more
marines scaled the seawall, one of them
carrying a twin-cylindered tank strapped to
his shoulders, the other holding the nozzle of
the flamethrower. As another charge of TNT
boomed inside the pillbox causing smoke and
dust to billow out, a khaki-clad figure ran out
of the side entrance. The flamethrower,
waiting for him, caught him in its withering
stream of intense fire. As soon as it touched
him, the Jap flared up like a piece of celluloid.
He was dead instantly but the bullets in his
cartridge belt exploded for a full 60 seconds
after he had been charred almost to noth-
ingness. It was the first Jap I had seen killed
on Betio — the first of 4,000, zing-zing, the
cartridge belt bullets sang. We all ducked
low. Nobody wanted to be killed by a dead
Jap.'

By mid afternoon on D+1, after carrier-
based planes had bombed and strafed the
enemy, A and B Companies of 1st Battalion
2/2, and what remained of Amey's 2nd
Battalion 2/2, now led by Lt-Col Jordan, a
total of no more than 135 men, managed to
cross the airstrip and occupy deserted enemy

Left: Marines crouch down as US destroyer shells oil dump which it has just set alight. *USMC*

Right: These British 8in Vickers naval guns had been captured by the Japanese at Singapore and were used on Tarawa for coastal defence. They were recaptured by Maj 'Mike' Ryan's men. *USMC*

Left: Marine sniping at enemy bunkers. *USMC*

positions on the south shore. Later Kyle, with C Company, fought through to join them and assumed command of these isolated units, Lt-Col Jordan reverting to his role of observer. The force arrived with little ammunition and no water or rations, and their precarious perimeter was soon under strong pressure from Japanese counterattacks which caused heavy casualties.

Over on the western end of the island near Red Beach 1 Schoettel had still not been able to land but one of his company commanders, Maj 'Mike' Ryan, had taken charge of the units ashore. He called down a heavy naval bombardment on to enemy positions on Green Beach and then moved the 3rd Battalion into the area. Resistance was mercifully light and Ryan had soon established a defensive line across the western end of the island about 200yd inland. This bold move could be said to be the first chink of light for the desperately hard-pressed Marine Command, and with this end of Betio now in the hands of the marines, and the enemy divided by the thrust to the south, the divisional commander decided to land part of the corps reserve on Green Beach, and 1st Battalion 6/2 (Maj Jones) was assigned this task. And, as it was reported that Japanese troops were escaping Betio by crossing to Bairiki Island to the east by a spit of sand, he ordered 2nd Battalion 6/2 (Lt-Col Murray) to land on Bairiki. This left 3rd Battalion (Lt-Col McLeod) as reserve, able to reinforce either landing teams. Both these landings were unopposed.

On Red Beach 3, in the meantime, men from Crowe's battalion, with K Company from Ruud's battalion, were still pinned down by the Japanese near the Burns-Philp wharf. A strongpoint at the base of the wharf, a reinforced steel emplacement, had interlocking fire with two others in the area, a large bombproof shelter and a machine gun nest. These mutually supporting positions were holding up the advance eastwards but by dusk Crowe had managed to advance his positions to the middle of the triangle made by the airstrip runways.

To the west of the main pier, the pocket of resistance on the borders of Red Beach 1 and Red Beach 2, which the previous day had caused such heavy casualties, was still active and was holding up the balance of Kyle's battalion moving to link up with Ryan and his men.

Despite these difficulties and the tragically heavy loss of life by late afternoon on the second day, Shoup felt sufficiently confident to send a heartening message to his divisional commander. 'Casualties many; percentage dead not known; combat efficiency: we are winning,' and with the critical phase of the battle now past Shoup handed over command of all troops to the division's chief of staff, Col Edson, and resumed command of his regiment, 2nd Marines. He was later awarded the Medal of Honor for his outstanding leadership and courage.

At dawn on D+2 1st Battalion 6/2, which had landed on Green Beach, was ordered to attack east along the southern coast of the island, pass through the isolated units now commanded by Kyle and continue the attack to the east. At the same time Hays was to try and reduce the pocket of resistance between Red Beach 1 and Red Beach 2, while over on Red Beach 3 Crowe and Ruud were to continue with their task of reducing the Japanese strongpoints by the Burns-Philp wharf. With Bairiki secured by Murray, artillery (2nd Battalion 10/2) was sent to the island and set up to fire on the Japanese occupying the tail of Betio. A definite shape to the marines' attack was now appearing. There was hard

fighting to follow but the desperate hours were over and the issue no longer in doubt.

Jones' move to the east along the south coast, supported by three light tanks of 2nd Tank Battalion, was accomplished with only light casualties and at 1100 hours he made contact with Kyle's group and continued to move east. At about the same time the last of the Corps' reserve 3rd Battalion 6/2 landed on Green Beach to support 1st Battalion's thrust eastwards which soon began to meet heavy fire. One enemy strongpoint, a turret-like emplacement near the beach, held up the 1st Battalion's advance for an hour and a half before it was destroyed by a medium tank. The other two scheduled attacks were now also meeting with heavy resistance. The pocket between Red Beach 1 and Red Beach 2, despite heavy pressure, continued to hold out, while at the other end of the invasion beach Crowe could only advance very slowly against the interlocking enemy strong-points. Then at 0930 hours the mortars supporting Ruud's K Company scored a direct hit on the machine gun nest and wiped it out, and at the same time a medium tank scored several direct hits on the steel pillbox and managed to neutralise it. Without supporting fire from these emplacements the large bombproof shelter now became vulnerable and fierce fighting developed round it. Engineers of the 18th Marines led by 1st-Lt Bonnyman Jr used flamethrowers and TNT to get to the shelter and eventually some managed to scramble to the top of it. An eye-witness, Master T/sgt Jim Lucas, a marine combat correspondent: 'Pfc Robert Harper, 22, Houston, Texas, and Sgt John Rybin, 25, Laurel, Montana, dashed forward with their flamethrowers while automatic riflemen covered them. At the entrance of the bomb shelter, Harper threw his flame on a Jap machine gun nest, charring three enemy marines beond recognition. He poured on more fire. There were screams inside the shelter and marines rushed forward to capture their objective.'

The Japanese counter-attacked but were driven off by Bonnyman and his flamethrower, and those trying to escape from the shelter were mown down. But in the fighting Bonnyman was mortally wounded. Later he was posthumously awarded the Medal of Honor.

With this emplacement finally overrun Crowe and Ruud were now able to advance their men as far as the eastern end of the air-strip before increasingly heavy opposition again halted them. They then dug in for the night and prepared for the counter-attack they knew must come from the still active and well-organised enemy units now compressed into the tail of the island. To the south of them Jones' men also dug in with McLeod's 3rd Battalion 6/2 behind them poised to pass through their lines the next morning and continue the advance. By the end of this the third day of fighting the marines had now confined the main Japanese resistance to the eastern end of Betio and a small pocket between Red Beach 1 and Red Beach 2. The end was in sight.

Above: A squad leader points to the spot where the Japanese are firing from while his men crawl forward. *USMC*

Above right: Making sure an enemy bunker has been cleared of the enemy. *USMC*

Right: Japanese dead littered the island when the battle was over. *USMC*

But though their strength was badly depleted there were still about 1,500 Japanese on the tail of Betio and it was looking as if the island's capture was going to take much longer than had been anticipated — and it had already proved to be a costly operation. A radio message sent to the corps commander by the divisional commander, who had now set up his Command Post ashore, highlighted the problem:

'Situation not favourable for rapid clean-up of Betio. Heavy casualties among officers make leadership problem difficult. Still strong organised resistance areas ... many emplacements intact on eastern end of the island ... In addition many Japanese strongpoints to westward of our front lines within our positions which have not been reduced. Progress slow and extremely costly.'

The expected counter-attacks did materialise that third night but with artillery support from 10th Marines, and gunfire from two warships, they were driven off after heavy hand-to-hand fighting which left 200 enemy dead in front of the marines' lines. A further 125 dead were found where the artillery bombardment had caught them assembling. The strongest of these counter-attacks came at 0400 hours, with the enemy assaulting the marines' lines screaming, 'Marines you die!' and 'Japanese drink Marine blood!' In places they managed to break through. 'The first we knew of the attack was the terrible screaming of the japs at the other end of the line,' said Lt Thomas who was acting company commander of one of the forward rifle companies when the attack was launched. 'It looked as though they were going to hit there but they were trying for a diversion and then they came up on against us with grenades and light machine guns and fixed bayonets. Their officers were swinging swords and about all we could see was shadows from gun flashes.'

Thomas called down artillery and naval gunfire support. He reported:

'That naval gunnery and our howitzers

61

impacting less than 75 yards in front of our line killed a lot of Japs, but they kept right on coming at us. Some of them broke through. I had a field telephone in my hands when I was rushed by the biggest Jap I've every seen, He yelled something I couldn't understand and charged me with his bayonet. We grappled for a few seconds and I managed to kick him off me and throw him to the ground. Then I picked up a .45 and finished him off.'

Thomas requested reinforcements but was told there were none. He was told to hold at all costs. He did.

A machine gun platoon supporting Thomas' men during this attack had also had to drive off the enemy in hand-to-hand fighting. Its commander, 1-Lt Walker, described a typical encounter:

'Two of the heavy machine guns had just been set up, and a third was being placed in position when the Nips opened up. The man on the number-one got off one burst before he was killed. A Pfc named Warfield took over and had just fired a couple of bursts when a Nip jumped in on him and stuck a bayonet in his thigh.

'Warfield's pistol was out of ammunition, so he couldn't shoot the Jap. He slugged him over the head with the butt. Two fellows in the squad ran over to help him. They were out of pistol ammunition, too, so they slugged the Jap with their pistol butts. They just about beat his brains out.'

These *banzai* attacks took their toll on the marines. But what remained of the Japanese garrison was bleeding itself to death with these suicidal assaults, and undoubtedly the annihilation of so many Japanese that night contributed to the sudden collapse of their resistance the next day — something Gen Smith could not have foreseen. It was a lesson future Japanese commanders were to take heed of when it came to defending other islands like Iwo Jima.

At 0800 hours on D+3 McLeod's men took over the attack to the east supported by artillery fire, two medium tanks and seven light tanks, while 1st and 2nd Battalions 2/2 were sent back to the beaches to help Hays' battalion with the one enemy pocket still holding out between Red Beach 1 and Red Beach 2. McLeod's progress was good until his I Company encountered a strong enemy strongpoint on the northern shore which held up the advance. However, it was found that the strongpoint could be by-passed and this was done with I Company being left to contain it, and the advance continued.

Suddenly, the enemy's resistance seemed to have petered out, and a rapid advance was achieved with various strongpoints being destroyed without coming under supporting fire. When these emplacements were later searched the many suicides discovered in them pointed to the fact that the enemy's morale had at last been broken. Many

Japanese had killed themselves by the complicated method of strapping their feet to the triggers of their rifles, placing the muzzles on their chests, and pulling the trigger by kicking it with their toes.

As McLeod's men approached the tip of the island a concentration of naval gunfire was put down ahead of them to prevent any Japanese escaping to Bairito from which the 2nd Battalion 6/2 had now withdrawn. By 1300 hours Betio had been completely overrun and the last Japanese pocket of resistance by the landing beach destroyed. Sporadic fighting did continue that night and later small bands of Japanese on Bairito and other smaller islands belonging to the atoll had to be hunted down and killed but the next day, 24 November, the Stars and Stripes was run up over the island of Betio. Alongside it — because Tarawa was a British possession — flew the Union Jack. The bitterest battle the marines had yet fought was over.

Left: Weary marines leaving Tarawa. *USMC*

Right: Two Japanese strongpoints: the upper shows a coconut log emplacement reinforced with a corrugated metal roof and coral sand, the lower a concrete emplacement strengthened by an out wall of coconut log stumps and coral sand.
Commando Association

The Normandy Landings

The landings of the Allied Forces in Normandy on 6 June 1944 needs little introduction here. It was the culmination of years of hard training and detailed planning. It employed the largest number of men ever known in this kind of operation and the troops, sailors and airmen, under the supreme command of Gen Dwight D. Eisenhower, came from many nations, including the United States, Great Britain, Australia, New Zealand, France, Holland and Belgium. By D+28 a million men of the Allied Armies of Liberation had landed in France.

But the first 48 hours were among the most vital ones for the Allies and the Royal Marines' part in establishing the bridgehead can be accurately assessed by covering those first two days ashore.

The Normandy landings on 6 June 1944 witnessed the largest gathering of Royal Marines ever to be used in one operation. Over 10,000 were employed in a wide variety of roles, some traditional, others entirely new to the Corps.

All the LCVs (Landing Craft Vehicle) and LCMs (Landing Craft Mechanised) which were used to ferry supplies to the beaches for the forward troops were manned by marines as were many of the LCAs (Landing Craft Assault) and LCI(S)s (Landing Craft Infantry, Small) which ferried the assault groups to the shore. Marines manned their usual turrets on the warships which bombarded the coast before the invasion and provided gun crews for the LCGs (Landing Craft Gun) and LCFs (Landing Craft Flak) which gave close fire support to the troops on the beaches. They also made up five of the eight Commandos (formed into two Special Services Brigades) which landed close behind the assault battalions, and provided specialised units. These special units included the Royal Marines Armoured Support Group, landing craft obstruction clearance units, Royal Marine assault engineers, beach parties, signallers, AA armament crews on the blockships, and personnel for running the naval ports, both natural and artificial.

The beaches at St Aubin sur Mer
after 48Cdo and Brigade HQ had
landed. *IWM*

Chronologically, it is right to describe first the hazardous role of those employed in getting the troops to the beaches, and supporting and supplying them. A typical example of the many acts of bravery committed by the marines involved in this task was that of Cpl Tandy. Tandy was coxswain of LCA 786, and when the steering wheel of his craft was carried away he acted as a human rudder in order to get the LCA with its troops to the beaches. The accident occurred when the LCA was being lowered from the parent ship, and though the beach was seven miles away Tandy immediately went over the stern and guided the rudder with his foot. Though waist deep in water most of the time and battered and bruised by the heavy swell Tandy got his craft to the shore on time and then returned it to the parent ship — still steering it with his foot, and his body half-submerged in the rough seas. For this exploit Tandy was later awarded the DSM.

Among those who went in with the first waves of assault troops were three members of the US Marine Corps acting as observers in an LCG. They kept an invasion diary which vividly describes what it was like to be there.

'Now we are closing in with the first assault wave. This is the moment the marine gun crews have been waiting for, and when Lt Hardwick (the marine gunnery officer), at his station on the bridge, gives the order to open fire, they fall to with a will. First they go after a concrete pillbox on the beach, just east of the mouth of the Seulles River and get a direct hit on it, then shift to a row of houses overlooking the foreshore. From the headquarters ship we get a signal that there is a strong point in a lonely house between the two villages in our sector. A ranging shot falls short. "Up 400," directs Hardwick on his phone, and the next salvo hits home. Meanwhile the assault waves are approaching the beach. Just before they touch down sheets of flame rise from rocket ships astern of us, clusters of rockets shoot over our heads and crash on the beach with a deafening roar.'

The air and naval bombardment before the first landings were so heavy that in some places the assault battalions were virtually unopposed. However, there were beaches, as will be seen, which were either unaffected by the bombardment or for some reason were not bombarded at all, and it was at these points that the RM Armoured Support Group Centaurs proved to be invaluable. Capt Scott, a troop commander in the Group, was one of the first ashore:

'The infantry came pouring ashore and our job was to fire over their heads and deal with any strong points which caused them trouble. Tank commanders had orders to have a go at these on their own initiative. Just in front of me was a large pillbox and were pumping shells into this as hard as we could go. Over on my left I saw my Troop lieutenant and another of my Troop tanks giving all they'd got to a large house almost surrounded by trees and from which machine gunners were making things uncomfortable for the leading infantry. I saw them get several direct hits on the building and they blew most of the top floors to pieces. The infantry were not idle all this time, they were attacking strongpoints and giving them hell with grenades, etc. I saw one commando race through a hail of bullets carrying a Bren gun right up to a pillbox, drop leisurely down, push the gun through the entrance and let fly.'

By far the largest group of Royal Marines employed during the landings were the five Royal Marine Commandos, 41 (Lt-Col T. M. Gray), 45 (Lt-Col Ries), 46 (Lt-Col Campbell Hardy), 47 (Lt-Col Phillips) and 48 (Lt-Col J. L. Moulton), whose job it was to clear the coastal defences along the whole length of the British beaches, Gold, Juno and Sword, in order that the assault troops which had preceded them could move directly inland and form a secure bridgehead.

On the extreme right flank 47 Commando (47Cdo) ran into problems before they had even landed for their LCIs began being picked off by a battery behind Arromanches, their landing beach. The CO ordered the landing craft to scatter and a new landing place was found about a mile to the west. One landing craft was sunk while this was being accomplished and during the run-in four more out of the 14 LCIs carrying the Commando were wrecked by the German defences, and only two eventually made it back to the LS(I) from which they had been launched. 'Perhaps we are intruding,' one marine was heard to remark philosophically. 'This seems to be a private beach.'

Eventually the Commando managed to get ashore but was scattered along a mile or more of beach. The plan was to rendezvous at Le Buhot church inland from the beaches and then march 10 miles or more across country, most of which was still in enemy hands, to an assembly area, Pt 72, a small hill about three miles south of Port en Bessin which was then to be attacked on the afternoon of D-Day. It was an extraordinarily boldly conceived operation that required great daring on the part of those involved, but the timing of it, after the near-disastrous landings, immediately began to go badly awry. The CO could not be found and the 2I/C, Maj Donnell, had some difficulty in collecting the scattered Commando and finding a way off the beach. A gap in the sea wall was found and the Commando made its way to the rendezvous and met up with the CO who had managed to get to Le Buhot by jumping on the ammunition sledge being towed behind a tank. Capt Isherwood, B Troop's commander, later described these first few hours vividly.

'The Lieutenant in charge of the craft shouted "dry landing" and I dashed forward carrying a total load of 90lb. To my great surprise I was walking on the seabed and wondering how long my breath would hold when abruptly the beach shelved and I surfaced about 20 yards from the West Wall. Everywhere was a shambles, probably from the first assault earlier. A huge gap in the wall led me off the beach and I was on a country road running parallel to the beach and leading to Arromanches. A machine gun opened fire and I threw myself into a ditch. For the first time I looked around and the whole of my Troop was crouched in the ditch behind me. Unfortunately most of them had

Below: LCTs (Landing Craft Tank) carried the RM Armoured Support Group to the beaches.
Commando Association

Above: Crews of S Troop of 5th Independent Battery, RM Armoured Support Group, preparing their Cromwell tanks at Emsworth, Hampshire, a few days before D-Day. *IWM*

discarded their weapons at the "dry" landing so I ordered them to arm themselves from the many bodies that were lying around. We avoided some mortar fire and made our way towards Le Buhot without confrontation. As we approached the church I saw a lone figure sitting on a bench who wanted to know where I had been and to get on with the advance. It was Colonel Phillips.'

The Commando now started on its 10-mile march through enemy held territory and arrived at La Rosiere at 1730 hours were it was decided to halt and assess the Commando's state and to reorganise. It was found that Q Troop commander had been killed on the beach, and that the Adjutant and two other officers had been wounded. 73 other ranks were missing; nearly all the Bangalore torpedoes and 3in mortar bombs had been lost, and the Heavy Weapons Troop had only one medium machine gun and one 3in mortar, which had lost its sight. Like B Troop, A Troop had lost practically all its weapons but unlike B Troop had not

been able to pick up enough, while Q Troop had lost nearly half its strength and Y Troop one third. However, X Troop was reasonably dry and well equipped as was HQ Troop though their wireless sets would not work.

Having reorganised, the Commando set off once more overrunning what scattered opposition they met from surprised German units and managing to collect sufficient enemy weapons from these encounters to equip A Troop. By the time they reached the assembly point, which was unoccupied except for a German first aid post, it was dark and the Commando dug in for the night.

Port-en-Bessin was defended by a triangle of strongpoints, one to the west and one to the east of the port on hills dominating it, and what appeared from the air reconnaissance map to be weapon pits to the south of the town behind the western feature. Before launching an attack on these three positions the CO sent out a fighting patrol to investigate the strength of the enemy in a nearby chateau at Fosse Soucy. It was decided that they were not in sufficient strength to interfere with the Commando's attack on Port-en-Bessin and in the afternoon, with fire support from a destroyer and the aid of a smokescreen the assault began. Before the Commando could enter the town to attack the two features, the weapons pit had to be cleared and this was successfully achieved by X Troop without casualties. A Troop, assigned the task of attacking the strongpoint on top of the western feature, led the way towards the port and was met by two policemen who offered to guide the troop through the back streets to the foot of their objective. While A Troop blew a hole in the wire and were preparing to move up the western feature B Troop, whose task it was to take the eastern feature, became pinned down at the edge of the harbour and became disorganised after suffering extensive casualties. Q Troop, or what remained of it after its heavy losses on the beaches, sent to reinforce B Troop, also became pinned down by accurate mortar fire from the eastern feature.

At first A Troop, led by Capt Cousins, seemed to be making good progress up the western feature but once the marines had climbed beyond the level of the rooftops they became targets for two flakships lying inside the eastern jetty of the harbour. They opened fire with 20mm cannon and the two right hand sections under Lt Wilson suffered especially heavy casualties, at least 11 marines being killed outright, and many more wounded. Wilson was hit and knocked unconscious while his batman lying at his side was killed and later A Troop's other subaltern, Lt Goldstein, was also wounded when he lay too close to a Bangalore torpedo with which he was blowing a hole in some wire near the top of the feature. With such heavy casualties, and still under fire, the troop now withdrew back into the town but Capt Cousins, undaunted by his experiences on the

western feature, immediately decided that he would try and assault the eastern feature. While he was collecting a small party of officers and men to find a route up to the strongpoint Maj Donnell collected another small party and went forward towards the harbour to locate the flakships and try to silence them with a PIAT. The flakships were located and the party took up firing positions in an abandoned enemy pillbox and poured fire on the two vessels, which soon had the German crews scrambling on to the jetty to surrender.

While Maj Donnell's party was locating and neutralising the two flakships Capt Cousins' party had found a broad track winding its way up the eastern feature to the strongpoint and decided, rightly, that as this was obviously the path the Germans used it would not be mined. The small party got as

Below: 45Cdo embarking at Warsash, Hampshire. *IWM*

Bottom: Map of where five RM Commandos landed.

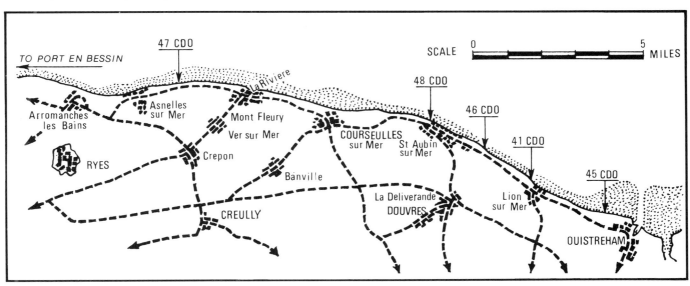

far as a low bank which ran across the hillside. Beyond it lay wire, and a well secured gate blocked the path. Above the line of wire ran a ridge along which the Germans had dug slit trenches whose occupants now began hurling stick grenades at the marines. However, as none of them dared stand up to throw, the grenades fell short and Cousins and his men were sheltered from the blast by the small bank. Cousins wanted to break down the gate and storm the strongpoint then and there, but was dissuaded from so doing by the others who pointed out that it would make more sense to get reinforcements from the port. The party then withdrew and Cousins reported to the CO who reinforced the party with more men from A Troop, and with men from Q Troop which was now under the command of Capt Vincent. He also arranged for supporting fire from some Bren carriers which had been used to bring ammunition from the landing beach, and from the one remaining 3in mortar. Smoke was laid and under its cover an enlarged party moved back up the path, cut the wire, moved through the now abandoned outer enemy defences, and then split in two. Capt Vincent moved to the right with his party while Capt Cousins took his party to the left. As dusk fell the two parties cautiously approached the crest. About 10yd from it they spread out and at about 2200 hours they were heard to give a loud cheer as they swept on to the summit of the feature.

Cousins' party came under heavy but inaccurate fire and overran several German positions before coming to the cliff path along which it had originally been planned that A Troop would attack. Wire protected the main part of the German strongpoint but Cousins found that a gap in it had been left where the path ran along the top of the cliff. He told Lt Wilson and the rest of the party to take shelter in the abandoned slit trenches while he went forward to explore the possibilities of advancing through the gap in

Top left: LCG(L) 1007: 'B' gun crew, all Royal Marines, firing on targets at Courseulles on D-Day. This picture was taken by a US Marine Corps photographer. *RM Archives*

Centre left: Technical Sgt Richard T. Wright, an observer from the US Marine Corps, with the Royal Marine gun crew of LCG(L) 831. *RM Archives*

Below left: Mulberry Harbour. The Royal Marines provided many of the personnel for running both the artificial and natural ports. *RM Archives*

Below: An LCF (Landing Craft Flak). The armament of these craft were mostly manned by Royal Marines. *IWM*

the wire. There was a good deal of confused firing and shouting and then the marine who had gone forward with Cousins crawled back and reported to Lt Wilson that Cousins was dead. In the meantime the men from Q Troop had wheeled to the right on reaching the crest, and, firing their weapons continuously from the hip as they advanced, they had covered about a 100yd when the Germans began surrendering. The prisoners included an English speaking Oberleutnant and he was taken by Capt Vincent to the other end of the strongpoint where Lt Wilson and his party were still pinned down and was instructed to persuade those still fighting to surrender. After some argument he succeeded in getting his men to surrender and the feature was at last in the hands of the marines.

The collapse of the defence of the eastern feature and the neutralisation of the two flakships in the harbour heralded the end of the Germans' fight to hold this vital port, and when morning came it was found that the strongpoint on the western feature had been abandoned during the night. However, while the fight for the port was still continuing, Germans from the chateau at Fosse Soucy had suddenly put in a counter-attack on the Commando's HQ Troop dug in on Point 72. Unfortunately, the marines had at first thought the advancing Germans were Americans as they were expecting to link up with the American army at any time. In the resulting confusion the position was overrun, 20 marines were taken prisoner, and several were killed or wounded. But when the CO sent a patrol to Point 72 the next morning the patrol found it had been abandoned by the enemy.

While 47Cdo was having a tough struggle to capture Port-en-Bessin, a few miles down the coast 48Cdo was also encountering stiff opposition. Contrary to what they had been told to expect, the enemy's defence positions had not been silenced when they landed half

an hour after the first assault had gone in. 'It was quite unrealistic to suppose the Canadians who went in at H-hour could silence them in the half-hour before we arrived,' the CO said later. The result of this miscalculation on the part of the planners was a near disaster.

The landing craft carrying Y and Z Troops were hit. Most of Z Troop was ferried ashore by an LCA but the rest had to try and swim for the shore, and many were drowned. The troop sergeant-major was carried west by the current for nearly a mile and was lucky to survive. Y Troop was picked up by an LCT, but this then bore them off to England and it was another two weeks before they were able to rejoin the Commando. Their commander, Maj Derek de Stackpole, however, plunged over the side and, despite being wounded in the thigh, reported for duty at the CO's command post. Smoke was now laid by the Commando from mortars set upon the surviving landing craft, and disembarkation began.

The Canadians had cleared the Commando's start line at the eastern end of St Aubin, and soon the village of Langrune was entered against only scattered opposition. The Commando's HQ was set up in a farmhouse and what remained of Z Troop was given the task of defending it while X Troop helped B Troop clear the seafront house of snipers.

At first all appeared to be going smoothly but then the Commando came up against the core of the enemy's resistance, a strongly fortified group of houses and X Troop reported increasing resistance with B Troop coming under heavy fire from the strongpoint. A sniper then killed its troop commander, and the troop's advance stalled. Two Centaur tanks of the RM Support Regiment were now sent forward to support B Troop in a push towards the crossroads at the eastern end of the strongpoint which was now seen to be protected by wire, trenches,

mines and a 5.5ft anti-tank wall. As B Troop started to advance again X Troop maintained its pressure down a parallel road at the western end of the strongpoint.

Initially, B Troop, supported by one of the tanks, made good progress, and some men managed to get under the wall of one of the houses belonging to the strongpoint but were then driven back by stick grenades. By this time the first Centaur had run out of ammunition and was replaced by the second which almost immediately hit a mine blocking the road for any other tanks. The Commando's attack on the strongpoint now petered out again and the CO was, as he put it, 'at a loss what to do about it', when he received orders from Brigade to stop the attack and arrange for the defence of the village as a counter-attack by German armour was expected at any time. However, the counter-attack did not materialise and the next morning the Commando renewed its attack on the strongpoint.

By now the resourceful CO had found an answer to the problem of overrunning the strongpoint: the anti-tank wall had to be destroyed so that his men could get into the fortified houses and clear them one by one. To do this he had to get the two Canadian M10 tank destroyers and the RM Support Group Troop Commander's M4 Sherman tank, which he now had under command, past the crippled Centaur. Fortunately, to the right of the stricken tank was an open field. It was mined but some of A Troop laid two Bangalore torpedoes under cover of smoke and these cleared a path through the mines which one of the M10s was able to follow. Once past the crippled tank the M10 moved back on to the road and started firing on the strongpoint and the anti-tank wall. Its high velocity anti-tank shells were very much more effective against the tough anti-tank wall than the Centaur's high-explosive shells had been. It soon began to crumble and then the Sherman moved up and blasted the

weakened structure until there was a big enough gap for the men of A Troop to rush the crossroads and storm the nearest house to the wall.

While A Troop were working their way through the fortified houses the CO had one of them blown up so that the rubble from it could be used to fill an anti-tank ditch which was the last tank obstacle before the seafront. Once this had been done the Sherman was brought forward so that it could fire along the promenade at Germans still holding out in the strongpoint, and the enemy's resistance soon began to crumble. The battle for the Langrune strongpoint had been won.

But the price had been a heavy one. Only five rifle troop officers out of 15, and 223 other ranks out of 500 who had embarked at Warsash, survived unscathed.

Though 48Cdo suffered heavily when landing 41Cdo, with whom 48Cdo was due to link up with at Petit Enfer on D+2, received severe casualties as well. As the Commando had been given two objectives the CO had split it into two parties. The first, under his own command, was to destroy a known strongpoint in Lion-sur-Mer; the second, under the command of the 2I/C, Maj Barclay, was to attack a suspected strongpoint in a chateau to the west of Lion-sur-Mer. The CO's party, consisting of A, P and Y Troops, managed to get off the beach and to the western end of the village where the CO established his HQ in the gardens of a villa. But the second party which had landed a few hundred yards apart from the rest of the Commando ran into a German artillery barrage which caused heavy casualties. Maj Barclay was killed and the troop commander of X Troop and several other officers were wounded. Caught on the open beach the men had to be persuaded to move on up the beach to the comparative safety of the dunes where the loose sand absorbed much of the blast. X Troop's sergeant-major Tom Morgan, eventually managed to get 19 of his men off

Below: RM Engineers clearing beach obstacles soon after H-Hour. Royal Marines formed half the teams employed in this task and were among the first men ashore. *RM Archives*

the beach. But many of the men, dead, wounded or simply dazed had be left behind.

The CO now took back the second party under his command and, having heard from villagers that the Germans had left at 0700 hours, ordered P Troop to occupy the supposedly deserted strongpoint in the village. Soon afterwards, however, P Troop reported it was being held up by snipers and LMG fire from houses on either side of the strongpoint and at the same time the South Lancashire Regiment, which had landed at H-hour, reported they were pinned down by fire from it.

The strongpoint dominated the main street of the village and was ingeniously disguised to look like an ordinary house. Windows and doors had been painted on the concrete exterior. Inside the fire positions all had accurate range maps of what was in their field of fire. In the grounds were three well concealed mortar positions — no more than holes in the ground — and an anti-tank gun. It was to prove a formidable obstacle for 41Cdo.

The CO now ordered B Troop to skirt the strongpoint and move up the road to the chateau making contact with the South Lancs on the way. He then sent Y Troop to support the South Lancs who had with them three AVRE tanks. No naval gunfire support was available as no wireless contact could be made with the warships lying offshore, but Y Troop and remnants of X Troop managed to get within 100yd of the strongpoint by advancing behind the three AVRE tanks. Cpl Mason of Y Troop said:

'I was behind the second tank, with our Troop Commander, Capt Howes-Dufton, and about five others. The attack went in and

Left: A group of A Troop, 45Cdo, before embarking at Warsash. Seated on the ladder on the right of the group is L Cpl H. E. Harden RAMC, the troop medical orderly, who was later to win the Victoria Cross. *IWM*

Below: LCI(S)s (Landing Craft Infantry, Small) like this one carried 47Cdo to shore. They were also used for landing the other Royal Marine Commandos. *Commando Association*

after the first tank was hit ours overtook it but then ours was hit too and so we moved off to the right down a lane with the idea of getting round to the right of the strongpoint. But at an intersection Capt Howes-Dufton was hit by a burst of fire from the left and then the Germans started throwing stick grenades over the walls at us, and we had to withdraw.'

The third tank was also hit and X Troop forced to take refuge behind a wall on the left of the road.

While the attack on the strongpoint was running into difficulties B Troop reported that it, too, was receiving casualties and that it was unable to advance to make contact with the South Lancs, nor could it make any attack on the chateau without more support. However, no further support was available, the only remaining 3in mortar having exhausted its ammunition when attacking the strongpoint. At 1310 hours A Troop, which had been sent round to attack the strongpoint from the south, reported it was under heavy mortar and rifle fire and that its troop commander, Capt Powell, was wounded. At the same time B Troop reported that an enemy force of about 60 was counter-attacking its position.

The situation for the Commando was now critical and the CO realised that to persist in his assault on the strongpoint could result in a general counter-attack from the enemy which could destroy his hard-pressed unit. 'There was quite a strong feeling,' commented the adjutant, Capt Taplin, 'that if a counter-attack had developed we could have been pushed back into the sea.' The CO therefore decided to concentrate the Commando along a line in Lion-sur-Mer east of the strongpoint and later in the afternoon, after contact had at last been re-established with the Navy, a destroyer shelled the strongpoint and the chateau for two hours. This eased the situation considerably and after the Commando had been reinforced with army units the village was surrounded for the night and the fighting died down.

The Commando's HQ was established for the night in an orchard outside Lion-sur-Mer and the night passed quietly. But on D+1 the Commando suffered a stroke of bad luck which had serious consequences. Early that morning a Heinkel bomber, under fire from a pursuing Spitfire, jettisoned its anti-personnel bomb on the Commando HQ killing the FOB and two others, and wounding the CO and 10 others. The adjutant now took command and 41Cdo then returned once more into Lion-sur-Mer to renew the attack on the strongpoint. But the Germans had withdrawn and no opposition was encountered either in the village or at the chateau and so the

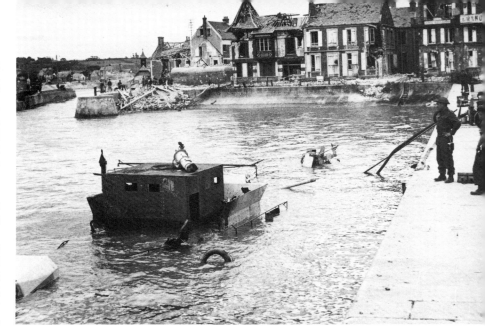

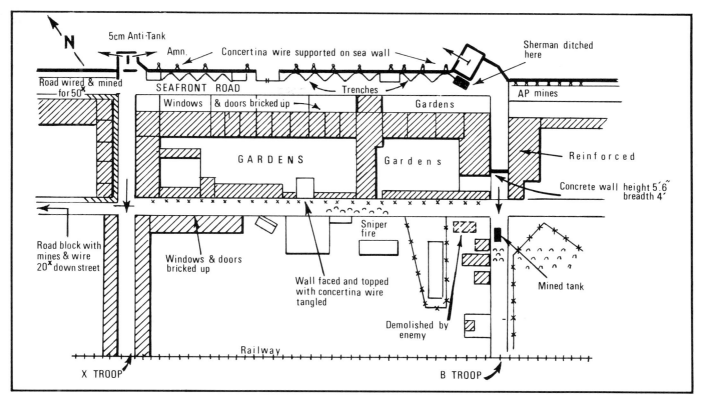

Top left: The remains of one of the flakships which caused so much trouble at Port-en-Bessin. *IWM*

Centre left: Royal Marines of Brig Leicester's 4th SS Brigade Headquarters coming ashore at St Aubin sur Mer. *IWM*

Bottom left: A marine of 48Cdo stumbles and falls during the landings. *IWM*

Above: Map of strongpoint at Langrune.

Commando made its way westwards as planned and linked up with 48Cdo. The next day it was sent five miles inland to contain a heavily fortified radar station at La Delivrande.

At the extreme eastern end of the British flank 45Cdo landed outside Ouistreham under heavy fire. Marine Thomas of A Troop wrote of the landing:

'Taking a quick look over the gunwhale of the craft, I saw a dark line stretched across the near horizon capped by a long pall of smoke. Out of this dark line little sparks of yellow light rippled and somewhere behind it came the noise of battle. I noticed that the flotilla of landing craft was now forming into a line for the run in on to the beach and that members of the crew aboard our craft were hurrying forward to man the ramps on touch-down. Various long spouts of water shooting up all around showed that the enemy was firing artillery at us. Suddenly I felt the craft surge forward and heard a voice over the intercom saying, "stand by to beach". There was a jolting along the whole length of the craft and that ever-so-calm voice saying, "down ramps, out troops!" An orderly rush forward towards the ramps took all the marines in its wave and rapidly we were struggling down the rather narrow ramps on to the sand of France. Halfway down the ramp I happened to look down into the waves beating on to the beach and there was a dead sailor with half his face missing moving up and down, back and forward with the motion of the tide. Then looking back for

a second towards the craft we had just left, I heard a loud crash, saw a flash of light and noticed a large dent appear in its bows. At the same time I saw to my horror two marines fall forward under the weight of their backpacks and the landing craft being driven by the surf right over them. On the beach there were soldiers lying about, some wounded, some still trying to dig themselves in, and others dead.'

Once clear of the beach which was mined and — despite the preliminary bombardment — still heavily defended by pillboxes which poured down flanking fire, the Commando passed through the lines of the assault battalion, the 2nd Battalion East Yorkshire Regiment, and assembled with the rest of Lord Lovat's 1st Special Services Brigade in a small wood some 1,100yd inland, the Commando's adjutant blowing 'gone away' on his hunting horn as a signal to muster. Soon afterwards contact was made with the 5th Parachute Brigade which had managed to capture intact the bridges over the Orne and the Caen canal and the brigade moved across them. The bridges came under increasing enemy sniper fire and later Lt-Col Rises, 45Cdo's CO, was wounded on one of the bridges and his 2I/C, Maj W. N. Gray, assumed command.

The role of 45Cdo within the task alloted the 1st Special Services Brigade was to capture the coastal battery at Merville — if this had not already been achieved by airborne troops — and then to move on and overrun Franceville Plage. As it was not clear whether the Merville battery had been taken or not, Lord Lovat ordered the Commando to proceed independently to it. Passing through the village of Sallenelles, contact with the enemy was made and then the Commando came under heavy fire from the battery. It later transpired that the airborne troops had in fact captured it but the Germans had later infiltrated back into it.

The CO was in the process of making out a plan of attack on the battery when orders from brigade came through not to attack it but to by-pass it and hold the village of Merville for the night. This was done but at 0300 hours further orders came through to rejoin the brigade at Le Plein in preparation for an attack of Franceville Plage, and this was launched at 1700 hours that day.

At first the advance went well but then two leading troops were held up as they approached the main enemy strongpoint in the town that dominated the main street from its northern end. An attempt by the commander of E Troop, Capt Beadle, and three marines of the troop's PIAT group to get a PIAT bomb into the strongpoint failed, and one marine was killed and another wounded. More casualties were suffered when an anti-tank gun fired at the HQ group which was moving up to see what was delaying the advance — the Commando was without any form of wireless communication as most of the sets had been destroyed in an earlier encounter with the enemy — and the RSM and one marine was killed, and several others wounded.

With the Commando's advance stalled and obviously heavily outnumbered an attempt was made to bluff the Germans into surrendering. But this proved fruitless and the Germans now began to infiltrate round the rear of the Commando to cut it off and push it on to the strong beach defences at the mouth of the Orne. Realising that the situation was critical the CO ordered his marines to withdraw from the centre of the town and to take up new defensive positions to the south on a grassy knoll which dominated the surrounding area. After some confused fighting in which the Germans tried desperately to cut off the Commando's line of retreat this was achieved, and patrols were sent out to bring in stragglers and the wounded. C Troop, the only troop in contact with the CO by wireless, remained separate, protecting the Commando's left flank.

The Germans, determined to press home their attack, now began to close in on the knoll and the CO ordered C Troop to counter-attack the enemy infiltrating round at the rear. The counter-attack was successful and after 15 minutes of fierce fighting the marines cleared a school building which dominated the Commando's rear. A defensive position was hurriedly organised by one of the section officers who took over command when the troop's commander, Maj Rushforth, was wounded and a German counter-attack was driven off. With his rear now secure the CO decided to withdraw to Merville under cover of darkness as ammunition was running low and there had been many casualties. This was successfully

Below: Lt-Col Moulton directing an M10 tank destroyer of 4th Battery RMASG during the battle for the Langrune strongpoint. *IWM*

achieved and at dawn relief signallers and additional wireless sets arrived from Brigade HQ, but no additional ammunition, nor any food, was received.

As the morning got lighter there was increasing enemy activity around Merville and at 0930 hours, after a heavy mortar concentration on the village, the Germans launched an attack from the direction of the battery but were beaten off. Then just before midday the Germans made a second attack, this time from the east and north, and the whole Commando was heavily engaged in repulsing it.

By now there were only two HQ officers left, the CO and the adjutant, and the latter produced the following duty officers' roster:

TO: CO
FROM: Adjutant

DUTY OFFICERS
You
Me
You
Me

The ammunition shortage was also acute by now. There were no 2in mortar or PIAT bombs at all and very little ammunition for the marines' personal weapons.

A third attack, supported by self-propelled guns which soon had the village on fire, was launched in the afternoon and it left the CO with no alternative but to withdraw, a move brigade had in any case sanctioned once night had fallen. Naval support fire covered

Top: Tanks of the RM Armoured Support Group moving inland; leading is an M4 Sherman, behind Cromwells. *IWM*

Above and right: The beaches at Ouistreham after 45Cdo landed. *IWM; RM Archives*

the marines' withdrawal from the fiercely burning village and a route was chosen that avoided known enemy positions. E Troop, however, soon found its way blocked by four machine gun posts which were flanked by a minefield on one side and the Merville battery on the other. With the enemy both behind and in front of it the Commando's situation looked grim indeed. E Troop was ordered to engage the machine gun posts while the CO tried to filter the rest of the Commando between the other German strongpoints.

Sgt Brown of E Troop, kneeling in the open without any kind of cover, dealt effectively with two machine gun positions with No 68 grenades fired from a specially strengthened rifle, while Marine Green maintained accurate covering fire with his Bren gun. Green lay in an exposed position being fed fresh magazines by his comrades who threw them up from a nearby ditch. He drew such accurate fire from the enemy that his weapon was hit twice, luckily without injury to either Green or the Bren. The courageous action of these two men greatly weakened the enemy's strength and Capt Beadle now decided on a direct assault to overcome any remaining opposition. The German posts were quickly overrun and two machine guns, two 81mm mortars and a motorcycle were captured, and as E Troop mopped up, the rest of the Commando slipped quietly through the German lines in single file.

The Commando rejoined the brigade just before dark and learnt that its stand at Merville had enabled the brigade to fight off a fierce counter-attack as it had diverted a vital part of the German force to the task of trying to take the village. The marines now had their first proper rest and their first hot meal since landing, and the next day took up defensive positions alongside other units from the brigade.

The fifth Royal Marine Commando to

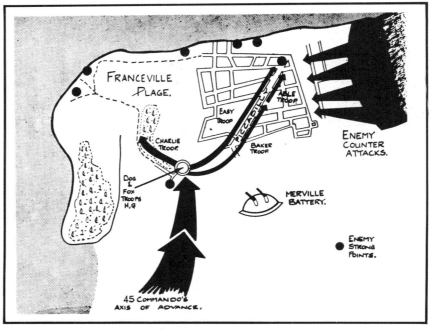

Top: Marines of 45Cdo in action by the side of the road. *IWM*

Above: Map of 45Cdo's advance on Franceville Plage.
Reproduced from Commando Men, *by kind permission Bryan Samain*

Left: Digging in by the glider landing area at Merville after the village had been cleared on D-Day. *RM Archives*

take part in the Normandy landings, 46Cdo, reverted to an infantry role as they were no longer required to take the batteries at Houlgate and Benerville and landed on D+1 with the task of taking the strongpoint at Petit Enfer. They landed unopposed at Bernieres at 0900 hours and with one troop of the RM Armoured Support Group under command, closed in on the strongpoint. It was known that the western defences of the German position were centred on an anti-tank gun positioned at a crossroads which was surrounded by a minefield and a labyrinth of wire and trenches. A and B Troops were each assigned one of the RM Armoured Support Group tanks and while B Troop with its Centaur drew the anti-tank gun's fire the tank with A Troop closed in and destroyed it. Marine Heaney of A Troop said:

'We moved forward to the strongpoint, and just as we reached a bend in the road the anti-tank gun fired at the tank. It missed. The tank withdrew back behind a house at the bend in the road and then after a few seconds moved forward again and fired at the anti-

tank gun. The first shot was smack-bang on the barrel of the gun killing the crew. A Troop then moved towards the strongpoint again and my Bren group took up position in a small garden about 150 yards from the strongpoint to help give cover to B Troop as they were making an attack on some trenches in front of the anti-tank gun. The Germans, their hands on their heads, soon surrendered.'

B Troop now moved round to the south side of the strongpoint and engaged the enemy, while A Troop negotiated the wire and the minefield and then managed to break into the stronghold from the seashore side. Once this had been achieved the enemy started to surrender and by 1800 hours all resistance had ceased, and the Commando then proceeded to occupy the remainder of the town.

The involvement of the Royal Marine Commandos — and other Royal Marine units — did not of course cease two days after the Normandy landings. But their initial tasks clearly displayed the tenacity and skill with which the marines have always fought.

Above: Men of 45Cdo with Bren gun watch for any enemy activity. *IWM*

Walcheren

Though the Normandy landings successfully established the Allied Armies on the Continent the Germans clung grimly to the Channel ports for as long as they possibly could knowing that without sufficient supplies the Allies would be unable to move far — and the lack of ports did at one point stop the Allied advance.

Then, on 4 September, the great port of Antwerp, 70 miles up the Scheldt River, was liberated but it could not be used by shipping while the banks of the Scheldt and the islands guarding the river's mouth were still in enemy hands. The clearance of most of these areas was achieved by the Canadian army. But the capture of Walcheren, the island that dominated the mouth of the Scheldt, became the task of a mixed British force, and the Westkapelle area, its most heavily defended part, the target of the Royal Marine Commandos.

Walcheren has been well described as a round cornered square about 10 miles across set so that its corners point NW, SW, SE and NE. Round its edges are dykes varying in height from 30ft in some places to about 200ft in others which protect the fertile land of the island which is below sea level. One of the biggest of these is the Westkappelle dyke just below the north-western rounded corner of the island.

Below left: The gap at Westkapelle. *Moulton*

This picture: LST approaching the Westkapelle gap. *IWM*

In preparation for the invasion of Walcheren, Lancaster bombers of the RAF blasted a hole in the dyke at Westkapelle, and another just north of Flushing. The North Sea quickly flooded the island, cutting the enemy's communications, inundating some of his gun positions and isolating others.

A three-pronged attack on the island was decided upon: from the east the 52nd Lowland Division would attack across the causeway which linked South Beveland to Walcheren; from the south 4Cdo, an army unit, would land at Flushing; and from the west a combined naval and military force — the latter consisting of Royal Marines of 41, 47 and 48Cdos — would attack the heavily defended coastline between Domburg and Flushing. The marines and 4Cdo were under the overall command of Brig Leicester RM and the naval force, which consisted of a support squadron of 25 landing craft adapted for support purposes, the battleship HMS *Warspite* and two monitors, HMS *Erebus* and HMS *Roberts*, were under the command of Capt A. F. Pugsley RN. Flotillas of LCTs and LCI(S)s would ferry the marines ashore while the support squadron, whose guns were manned by marines, engaged the batteries at close range.

The combined assault on the island was fixed for 1 November 1944 and was to be preceded by an intense aerial and naval bombardment. The plan was for 41Cdo, commanded by Lt-Col E. C. E. Palmer, to land north of the hole torn by the bombers at Westkappelle and move up the coast to Domburg, capturing two of the four main enemy batteries, W15 and W17. This accomplished they would then move on through Domburg to capture two further German batteries, W18 and W19. At the same time 48Cdo, commanded by Lt-Col J. L. Moulton, was to land south of the gap and clear the coast as far as the village of Zoute-lande including the capture of battery W13. Once Zoutelande had been reached 47Cdo, commanded by Lt-Col C. F. Phillips, would pass through them and continue to clear the coast — which included the capture of W11 and a smaller battery, W4 — until they met up with 4Cdo north of Flushing.

All three Commandos were to use American amphibious LVTs — the British called them Buffaloes — and the lighter amphibious Weasels as it was hoped they could be used on the flooded inland waters to outflank the enemy as well as on the difficult hilly sand dunes. It did not work out like that but, as the CO of 48Cdo commented, it was

Above: Amphibians landing in the Westkapelle gap. *RM Archives*

an improvement on the Normandy landings. 'This was the way to land — dry shod, plenty of fire power, very few casualties, and my wireless set with me.'

The landings, however, were hazardous in the extreme for not only did they take place right under the muzzles of the German guns but the marines had practically no beach to land on. Opposing them and overlooking the Scheldt were the four main batteries of large calibre guns some of which were housed in concrete casements of the heaviest kind and surrounded by smaller batteries, flak positions, pillboxes, weapon pits, minefields and barbed wire. For some it was to be the toughest fighting of the war.

The support squadron, too, had an unenviable task, luring the main German batteries into engaging them and not the landing craft ferrying the marines ashore, and there were many acts of bravery by the naval crews and the marine gunners of the LCGs and LCFs that fought that day. But there were two craft in particular whose crews performed an especially hazardous role. They were LCG(M)s, whose main armament consisted of two 17pdr guns mounted in 4.5in armoured plated turrets. They were the first of their kind in service and had been specifically designed for assaulting gun positions on the beaches of Japanese-held islands in the Pacific. These two craft were to precede all the other seaborne units and their specific task was to engage batteries W13 and W15 situated on either side of the gap at

Westkappelle. They were to be driven ashore right under the batteries and engage them at point-blank range with their high-velocity guns.

As the two craft closed to within about a mile of the coast the order was given to open fire on individual targets with armour piercing shells. Both LCG(M)s were ballasted down with special tanks almost to deck level and just before grounding a kedge anchor was let go so that once the ballast tanks had been blown the craft could haul themselves quickly away from the dyke once their tasks had been completed. By the time LCG(M)101, with its two 17pdr guns controlled by Lt Tiffin RM and Sgt Russell-Taylor RM, had beached on the dyke north of the gap right under the muzzles of W15 it had already been hit several times, and the crew now found themselves engaging the enemy at point-blank range as a manuscript account in the RM Archives vividly describes: 'Not more than fifty feet separated the ship from the nearest gun and at this point machine guns in armoured cupolas in the dyke walls could be heard firing and hits from the bullets could be felt on the walls of the gun turrets. Several guns along the dyke walls were unaccounted for and they were just able to bear round and score several hits on the port quarter just below the water line.

'Inside "B" Turret on the port side, firing continued for several rounds after the ship struck the beach but ceased when the periscope sight of the gun commander was shot away leaving him blind to outside events. Bullets from the machine guns on the dyke walls started to penetrate into the turret having been deflected upwards from the deck outside. Other bullets came into the turret through the sighting ports where the gun layer and gun trainer sat behind their telescope sights. Both sights were shattered with the gun layer receiving several fragments to the side of the head throwing him backwards. Further bullets coming up through the deck from outside hit him in the hands and others ricocheting from the angled walls of the turret, buzzed around inside like insects. Several bullets then struck the gun leader in both arms causing him to fall sideways in a faint under the breach of the gun.

'The sighting ports were then blocked with metal covers to prevent further entry of bullets and the deck grille leading down into the magazine was pulled up. The injured gun loader was then passed down into the arms of the magazine crew who had been horrified to see blood dripping down on them from above.

'Replacing the deck grille and removing the sight port covers, the remaining gun crew were then able to get the gun back into action with the gun commander doing the work of the gun loader.'

Despite being in so close that some of the larger guns could not depress sufficiently to it, the LCG(M) was being repeatedly raked by machine gun fire and after firing about 50 rounds at W15 — none of which pierced the heavy concrete — the captain decided to withdraw and attack another part of the beach. The ballast tanks were blown and a party sent aft to haul in the kedge. The party, however, was wiped out by machine gun fire which also severed the kedge's wire hawser. The craft began to back away from the beach but almost at once it started to sink by the stern and the order was given to abandon ship. Within minutes LCG(M)101 went down.

LCG(M)102 fared even worse. She received a direct hit after beaching by W13 and was later seen to be in flames and broached-to. There was only one survivor, a marine, who said the craft had probably been hit by a flamethrower.

The batteries, however, did not escape unscathed. W15 was hit by shells from HMS *Roberts* and then strafed by rocket-firing Typhoons. This combined attack crippled two of its guns and must have severely reduced its efficiency just at the time the invading force was a prime target. W13, for some reason which has never been determined, ran out of ammunition at 1017 hours, a matter of minutes after 48Cdo had landed. It is possible that 48Cdo's swift advance and attack on it prevented further ammunition being brought up for it.

The courage of the crews of the support squadron allowed the first waves of the Marine Commandos to land relatively unscathed and on the north side of the gap 41Cdo landed successfully on the dyke. One

Below: LCG(M) 101 sinking by the stern. *Commando Association*

Survivors being taken aboard
LCI(S). *Commando Association*

of the leading landing craft was hit killing the section commander. But the section sergeant, Sgt Musgrove, immediately took command and single-handedly knocked out the section's first objective, a pillbox which was pouring heavy fire along the dyke. This action enabled the Commando's first wave, consisting of B, P and the MMGs of S Troop under the command of the Commando's 2I/C, Maj Peter Wood, to move quickly away from the beach. B Troop advanced into the remains of the village of Westkappelle, now knee-deep in water, while P Troop and the MMGs of S Troop turned left and began to bring W15 under small arms fire. This accomplished, the balance of the Commando landed along with a detachment of tanks. (Out of a total of 20 tanks and four armoured bulldozers only a handful ever got into action. Most got stuck in the clay and soft sand, and some never even landed.) A Troop, assigned the task of taking the tall, solidly built Westkappelle Tower, managed, after a brief skirmish, to bluff its occupants into surrendering and before long the devastated village was in the hands of the marines. An attack was now planned on W15 and a way found round its flank between the dyke and the floods. An assault was then launched by Y Troop, commanded by Capt Peter Haydon, with P Troop giving supporting fire. After half-an-hour's sharp fighting the battery's garrison surrendered and 120 prisoners were taken. Both troops then advanced as far as the lighthouse which marked where the land turned north-east taking prisoners all the way, but then the Commando was halted by the brigade commander until the situation south of the gap became clearer.

On the south side the battle was not going as well as it had for 41Cdo to the north. B, X and Y Troops of 48Cdo landed at 1005 hours on the southern shoulder of the gap with relatively few casualties but the second wave bringing in the rest of the Commando came under much heavier and more accurate fire. One LCT received a direct hit, the shell bursting against the LVT (Buffalo) carrying

the MMGs. The driver and the wireless operator were killed and two members of the MMG detachment badly wounded. Capt Linnell, the Support Troop commander, had a narrow escape. 'The 6in shell landed in the driver's compartment and only 18in in front of my nose. The blast blew me backwards and I lost my beret, and all the hair on my head was burned off. For the first time in many years I had no moustache. No one recognised me.' He had to swim ashore. Even when ashore the second wave was, initially, harder hit, many of their amphibians being destroyed by mines or shell fire. And then the leading troops, after swiftly overrunning the radar station and two strongpoints, came up against the defences of W13 and immediately ran into trouble.

In order to maintain the momentum of the Commando's advance, Maj Derek de Stacpoole, commanding the leading troop at the time, decided to launch an unsupported attack on the battery along the narrow strip of sand which at this point was the only ground remaining between the sea and the inland floodwater. As speed was essential to

Top: LCG(M) 102 *Neighbour*

Above: Amphibians of 41Cdo being driven ashore from LST on north side of gap. *IWM*

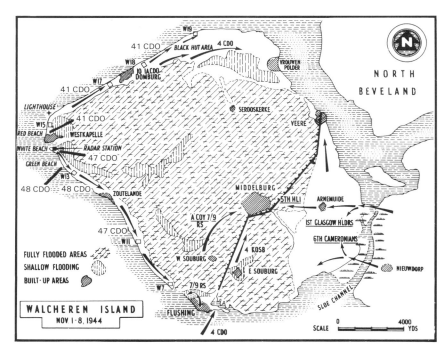

Above: Map of Walcheren and where RM Commandos landed.

had been established with the operation's command vessel, HMS *Kingsmill*, which in turn could arrange for timed barrages to be put down by Canadian artillery on the other side of the Scheldt. The CO therefore decided to return the few hundred yards to Brigade HQ and arrange for both artillery and RAF strikes on W13. But while he was away disaster struck and when he returned he found the forward troops, which had been deployed ready to attack the battery once the bombardment was over, had been heavily mortared. Z Troop, which had been detailed by the CO as the assault group, had no one above the rank of corporal unwounded and there were many other casualties amongst the other two forward troops. However, an A Troop Bren gunner had managed to silence the 81mm mortar which had caused all the damage, and B Troop was now brought forward to take over Z Troop's role. The artillery barrage began at 1545 hours and was succeeded by Typhoons which dropped 500lb bombs and raked W13 with cannon fire all within about 200yds of the waiting Commando. J. L. Moulton described the next stage in *Battle for Antwerp* (Ian Allan Ltd, 1978).

'As the last aircraft completed its dive, B Troop, covered by 2in mortar smoke and by A Troop in a fire position where the narrow dunes luckily broadened slightly to allow some degree of flanking fire, went forward over the dunes, crossed a minefield, which like others crossed earlier had been made ineffective by drifting sand, and entered the battery position. X and Y Troops followed B, and soon the battery control position and three of the four casements were in the hands of the Commando. Later, patrols reached the fourth casement, and, searching the admin-

the whole operation this was almost certainly the right as well as the most courageous decision. But the attack was driven off, Maj de Stacpoole was killed, and many of his troop wounded.

With the enemy's wits returning to him after the ferocity of the bombardment, and with the Commando's advance now held up by W13, the CO of 48Cdo immediately sought fire support for a new attack. But his only direct contact was with HMS *Roberts*, whose guns were insufficiently accurate for really close support, and with the southern support group which, by this time, had been virtually wiped out. However, a brigade link

istrative buildings below the dunes, brought in about seventy prisoners. By then it was dark, and a single Oerlikon still firing at the far end of the position was left until morning. Through the cold, moonlit night the men of the Commando cleaned weapons, carried up ammunition, patrolled, ate the scanty rations they had in their pockets, slept or shivered, and made ready to advance when it grew light.'

While 48Cdo were attacking W13 41Cdo had been ordered to continue its advance on battery W17 and Domburg. W17 had been continuously battered by HMS *Warspite's* 15in guns throughout the day but it was still firing intermittently at the Westkappelle beaches where supplies were being brought in and the wounded taken off. However, once attacked by the marines the battery's garrison soon surrendered but X Troop, covering the advance out on the dunes to the left, ran into an ambush in the fading light. Lt Jewers who was in command of the leading section commented:

'We seemed to be in a defile and, as we moved forward, all hell broke out. We were right under a strongpoint manned by fanatics (or drunks!) judging by the yells, etc, and they showered us with flares, stick bombs, and automatic fire from 20 or 30 yards range, or so it seemed. We ducked into a slit trench and Brind-Sheridan (the Troop Commander) crawled up. He told me to go back and to extricate my section while he went the other way. As we moved there was another outburst which killed Brind-Sheridan and his MOA (batman). I couldn't raise anybody on the radio so we decided to make a run for it back to the Troop. We were lucky in losing, I think, only one man in this exercise. I still

Top: An LCT(R) giving supporting fire. *IWM*

Above: Men of 47Cdo approaching the beach south of the gap. *RM Archives*

Below: 47Cdo disembarking. *RM Archives*

could not raise anybody on the radio and so took command of X Troop and ordered a withdrawal to cover the strongpoint from the south-west while I contacted the CO.'

While X Troop was extricating itself P Troop had found its way into Domburg illuminated by fires started by the shells of HMS *Warspite* and moving right through the village attacked and captured the German HQ in the Bad Hotel.

South of the gap 48Cdo's advance to Zoutelande began the next morning at 0630 hours. Only occasional Spandau fire, and a determined rifle grenadier who was quickly silenced, was encountered, and by 1100 hours, after clearing two enemy positions on the dunes and winning a short fire fight with the garrison in the village, A Troop entered Zoutelande and then pushed on beyond it to secure the high dunes to the south. A Troop were now ordered to halt their advance so that 47Cdo could take over, and just before

1300 hours the first units of 47Cdo passed through it and moved on down the coast towards W11.

So far 47Cdo had not had much luck. After being ordered to land at midday three of the four LCTs carrying the Commando were hit by shells and then there was confusion as to the actual landing point. As a result only one LCT unloaded its amphibians in the correct place, south of the gap, the others either moving over to the north or simply lowering their ramps without beaching at all. However, once the amphibians were in the water at least one section commander made the decision to make for the northern edge of the gap to avoid the shelling and the confusion to the south. Y Troop was one that landed to the north deliberately but then quickly crossed to the south. As a result it was one of the first to reach the assembly point and had few casualties. On the other hand half of B Troop had been lost when one of the LCTs

had been hit and when the Commando finally assembled at 1900 hours it was found there was only one MMG and two 3in mortars, and that a lot of other equipment had been lost. Most of the Weasels had either sunk or been abandoned, and most of the men were soaked through. It was not a promising beginning.

But despite these setbacks 47Cdo was eager to take over the advance from 48Cdo the next morning, and when it did so, it soon overran the first strongpoint it encountered beyond Zoutelande, and moved on towards W11. The land around this battery had not been as affected by the flooding as elsewhere and behind the two parallel lines of high undulating dunes which limited visibility in any direction to not much more than 50yds was an unflooded area of land on which were a few scattered houses called Klein Valkenisse and some German barracks. The whole area was isolated by an anti-tank obstacle consisting of mines, dragon's teeth and a broad ditch, which extended from just north of W11 down to and including Flushing.

The advance up to this obstacle had gone well, with the Germans surrendering without putting up much resistance, but then suddenly Q Troop which was in the lead came under heavy and accurate fire from a ridge beyond the anti-tank obstacle and from the German barracks to its left. Caught on top of the open dunes by this heavy concentration of mortar and machine gun fire the troop suffered severe casualties including its troop commander, Maj Vincent, who was shot through the eye. The advance was halted and Q Troop thrown into complete confusion. X Troop, which was following Q,

Top: Marines of A Troop 41Cdo advancing towards the Westkapelle tower. *IWM*

Above: Marines in the shattered remains of Westkapelle. *IWM*

Right: Bringing back prisoners to the beachhead. *IWM*

also came under fire and its commander was wounded when he went forward to assess the situation.

The rest of the Commando now halted while the CO made a plan of attack which would bring the Commando up to W11 which lay about a thousand yards distant. At 1550 hours he ordered Y Troop to take over the attack and assault three intermediate positions before attacking the battery itself. 'My plan,' wrote the CO, 'was to attack on a one troop front. Y Troop to lead, closely followed by A Troop. B Troop's task was to follow A and mop up. X Troop was in reserve.' He added succinctly: 'Q Troop had disintegrated.'

Y Troop now advanced through Q Troop's casualties lying on the dunes, was held up by artillery fire, but then moved forward again and captured two of the intermediate strongpoints before being checked. A Troop then went through Y but was also held up and was soon joined by Y again and from then on the remnants of these two troops fought as one under Y Troop's commander, Capt Flower, until he was wounded. They moved forward for the attack on W11 itself, an attack described in *Battle of the Dyke* (a manuscript in RM Archives, Eastney 7/19/3):

'Captain Flower walked about encouraging his men with almost casual disregard for the fire, though in full view of the enemy, urging them forward. A cold, strong wind was blowing, whipping up the sand in a stinging spray in the faces and eyes of the advancing marines, clogging their automatic weapons. But they plodded forward, slipping and slithering in the soft heaps of sand until within 30 yards of the first line of defences. Here Captain Flower was wounded in the chest and arm by a German stick grenade, but, under close fire from weapons of all kinds, he rushed the first German weapon pit, killing the three men manning it with his Tommy gun.

'The Germans fought stubbornly and bitter hand-to-hand fighting took place. The Troops following closed up with the leaders but suffered heavily, their Commanders, Captains M. G. Y. Dobson and J. D. Moys, being hit. The Germans counter-attacked and Captain Flower and his men were forced back into a gulley below the first battery position. That indomitable officer was again hit by a bullet but, weak from loss of blood, he sustained the courage and resolution of the men with his cheerfulness. He was magnificently supported by Sgt-Maj J. P. England, who attacked a machine gun post alone, seizing a Bren gun from a dead man and struggling up a soft, sandy slope, firing from the hip as he went. He killed two of the defenders and the third fled. His Bren ran out

of ammunition so he took up a German light machine gun to tackle another position thirty yards further on, killing three more Germans and taking two prisoner.'

Despite the courage and tenacity with which this attack was pressed home the marines could not break into the battery. Night was now falling, all the troop commanders were wounded, all the wireless sets were either inoperative or lost, and the Commando was widely scattered and disorganised. Lt Winter, Y Troop's only other officer, had been stunned by a shell, but he now came forward and collected the scattered remnants of Y Troop and joined forces with Lt Lloyd and a small party of B Troop. Together they tried to move round to the seaward side of the battery. 'Then I saw a German patrol coming down the beach towards us,' said Lt Winter, 'and it became very apparent that unless we pulled back we were going to be cut off.'

To make matters worse a German position to the Commando's rear was stubbornly holding out and preventing any supplies or reinforcements being brought forward. Faced with this situation the CO had no alternative but to break off the attack and fall back and consolidate for the night. 'When it was getting dark,' he wrote, 'I realised that the attack had failed and I had no reserve left. My chief concern was to regain control of the fighting troops and to get a clearer picture of what shape they were in and to find out as fully as I could where the enemy were, and where they were not.' In short the situation for 47Cdo was not far short of being desperate, a fact the CO fully acknowledged when he later began an account of the attack on W11 with the words that 'a complete and

Above: Lt-Col Palmer, CO of 41Cdo, with his 2I/C Maj Wood, watching one of the two surviving gun tanks in action east of Domburg. *Eekman Collection*

Above right: Men of 10 (IA) Commando in action north of Domburg. *Eekman Collection*

Right: The brigade commander, Brig Leicester RM conferring with Lt-Col Palmer, CO of 41Cdo, on his left. On the right is the 2I/C of 41Cdo, Maj Wood. *RM Archives*

Bottom right: This 3.7in British gun was installed in Battery W15. *IWM*

accurate account can never be written so great was the confusion.'

However, the situation was eased somewhat by the initiative of the adjutant, Capt Paul Spencer, who set about reorganising the men into an all-round defensive position for the night. Soon afterwards a very worried brigade commander arrived at the CO's Tac HQ and urged him to continue the attack that night by the light of the newly risen moon. But the CO refused to attack before he and his men fully reorganised and the brigadier concurred with this decision. He insisted, however, that 47Cdo needed additional firepower and A Troop, 48Cdo, was sent forward for this purpose. During the night a German patrol, probably the one seen by Lt Winter but perhaps one consisting of troops from the barracks, attacked the Commando and demanded its surrender, but the marines drove the Germans off without difficulty, and when morning came the CO planned a fresh assault once his men had been properly reorganised for an attack.

A heavy artillery bombardment was brought down on the battery and while Maj Donnell covered the left flank with the remains of Q and Y Troops, A Troop, 48Cdo, gave enfilading fire from the inner lines of dunes, the rest of 47Cdo pressed home its second attack on the battery. The Germans fought bitterly and co-ordinated control of the attack was soon lost. The Commando regrouped into small parties and eventually one group of marines, accompanied by some Dutch commandos from 10(IA) Commando, got into the casemate of one gun. The adjutant then collected some more men and led an attack up a steep sandy slope right into the centre of the battery while

the marines around the casemate gave covering fire. Once inside the battery the adjutant's party was able to fight its way along a maze of communication trenches and underground passages to the other casemates, acting, as the adjutant aptly described, like ferrets after rabbits, and within three-quarters of an hour the whole battery was in their hands. Many of the prisoners they took were half-crazed from the intensity of the bombardment.

Only one position, W4, an administrative post with smaller coastal guns south of W11, now continued to hold out and when the CO sent men from A and B Troops to capture it the Commando's momentum slowed for the first time that day. It was soon realised that the remaining Germans had been pushed back to W4 and were now consolidated in one position. 'It then became a question of bluff,' commented Capt Spencer who led the party down to W4. 'The Germans couldn't see what our strength was and we had no idea what theirs was. We came under fire and everyone took cover out of sight and I found myself right at the entrance to the battery. I saw what looked like an officer and shouted at him in German that there was a considerable army behind me and that there was no point in fighting on and that he should surrender.' The adjutant then asked to speak to the German commandant and when he appeared Spencer urged him to tell his men to throw down their arms. After some prevaricating the German commandant agreed.

Top left: The remains of Battery W15. *Eekman Collection*

Centre left: A dead German who had been manning one of the batteries. *RM Archives*

Left: Battery W17 consisted of four 8.7in guns. The control tower can be seen in the background. Although their open casements made them more vulnerable to gunfire they survived over 300 15in shells from HMS *Warspite. IWM*

Above: The crew of LCT 469 erecting tents and shelters after their ship had been wrecked. *IWM*

He was then taken to the CO of 47Cdo to whom he handed over his pistol saying to Lt Winter, who was acting as interpreter, 'Tell your general that if he does not think I have fought well, here is my pistol, he can shoot me with it now.' When this was translated the CO later commented that he was so relieved he could have embraced him. Instead he ordered him to call out his men for them to be disarmed.

Rather to the consternation of the handful of marines no less than 180 Germans came out from various positions heavily outnumbering the Commandos. However, the Germans were quickly disarmed and marched away.

Although the batteries overlooking the Scheldt had now been overrun, and the minesweepers were now able to start operating, there was still some fierce fighting to be done north of Domburg to capture the last two batteries in that area, W18 and W19, and to clear the Germans from a feature in between them called the Black Hut where there were known to be several enemy held emplacements. On 4 November, therefore, 41Cdo, which had been moved south of the gap at Westkapelle in case it was needed to capture W11, moved back to the north to Domburg where it rejoined the three troops

that had been left there to repel any German counter-attack. An assault on W18 was launched on 5 November by Y Troop. Its commander, Capt Haydon, had won the DSO in Italy at the early age of 19 and now he said to a companion before leading the attack, 'this time a VC or bust.'

The assault went in despite heavy fire but Haydon and one of his section officers was killed and the other section officer was wounded, and the troop was temporarily led by Cpl Nightingale who subsequently was awarded the DCM for his bravery during this action. A Troop following up pressed home the attack and the battery was cleared, though mopping up continued for much of the night.

The next morning the advance continued but only slow progress was made through the minefields, and it was not until the afternoon of 7 November, after rocket attacks by Typhoons, that the Black Hut area fell to the marines. By now the rest of the brigade had reached the area, but before the advance could be reinforced the Germans defending W19 surrendered.

The battle for Walcheren was over and on 26 November the Scheldt was opened to Allied shipping and supplies began to flow to the armies pressing in on Germany.

Iwo Jima

By the beginning of 1945 the noose around Japan's neck was beginning to be pulled tight. Carrier-borne US aircraft were striking with increasing frequency at bases in Japanese territory while land-based B-29s were, after the fall of Saipan in June 1944, able to bomb Japan itself. The US Marine Corps and US Army had effectively cleared or isolated the enemy in most of the outlying Pacific islands. The time had come to strike a blow at Japan's inner ring of defences so that a path could be cleared for the final strike against mainland Japan. Iwo Jima was a main link in this last-ditch defensive ring. Smash Iwo Jima with its three airstrips and the chain holding closed the door to Japan itself would fall apart.

This picture: Marines take cover behind a tank as it advances against the enemy on D-Day. *USMC*

Iwo Jima — Iwo means sulphur and Jima means island — was a volcanic strip of pear-shaped land five miles long and two and a half miles across at its greatest width. It lay within 660 nautical miles of Tokyo. At the southern end was a 500ft extinct volcano called Mt Suribachi and up the centre of the island, like a backbone, were the three air-strips, the third being incomplete. The ground at the southern end was mainly sandy but in the north where sulphur fissures were still active it was volcanic ash which made foxholes too hot to live in. Rations could be cooked by simply burying the cans in the ground. The whole place stank like a bad egg and the terrain was pockmarked with caves, rocky ridges and deep ravines. Combined with this hostile geography was an extensive and intricate Japanese defensive system. Together they were to make Iwo Jima a living hell for the invading marines.

'In describing Jap positions or defensive organisations of the ground,' wrote Maj Heinl who was there, 'many terms lose their meaning. There were no lines, no perimeter. Iwo was one solid, co-ordinated defense, the density of which has never been exceeded by any objective taken by American arms.'

Defending this honeycomb of concrete, steel and rock were 22,000 troops of the Imperial Japanese Army and Navy under the command of Lt-Gen Kuribayashi. Although he asked for reinforcements during the course of the battle, Kuribayashi never expected to receive any; and though, again during the battle, he wondered where the Japanese navy and air force were, he knew only too well he would never receive much help from them for they had practically ceased to exist except as suicide units. He knew he was there, alone and isolated, until he won or lost. He did not have much doubt about what would happen. 'The island is the front line that defends our mainland,' he said before the marines landed, 'and I'm going to die here.' He did, and so did the vast majority of the troops under his command. But the tragedy of Iwo Jima was that for every Japanese who died an American marine was killed or wounded.

'The enemy could have displaced every cubic inch of volcanic ash on this fortress with concrete pillboxes and blockhouses, which he very nearly did,' commented the 3rd Marine Division's commander, Maj-Gen Erskine, 'and still victory would not have been in doubt. What was in doubt, in all our minds, was whether there would be any of us left to dedicate our cemetary at the end, or whether the last marine would die knocking out the last Japanese gun and gunner.'

It was as bad as that. It was to be the marines' costliest battle and the hardest won. It was also the battle by which they will always be remembered.

On 19 February 1945, after eight months of intermittent, then daily, and finally continuous, aerial and sea bombardment, two marine divisions assaulted the island. The Vth Amphibious Corps (Maj-Gen Harry Schmidt) had been given the task of taking Iwo Jima and three marine divisions were assigned for the operation: the 4th Division (Maj-Gen Cates) and the 5th Division (Maj-Gen Rockey) were to provide the assault troops with the 3rd Division (Maj-Gen Erskine) being held in reserve. The 3rd and 4th Divisions were seasoned fighters, having taken part in the Marianas and

Saipan-Tinian campaigns respectively, while the 5th Division was built round a core of battle-experienced men, survivors of earlier campaigns like Guadalcanal and Tarawa. In all 100,000 troops were to be used in the assault and then garrison of Iwo Jima, 60,000 of them marines.

As dawn broke on 19 February a vast armada of 800 ships surrounded Iwo Jima. From 0640 hours to 0805 hours the US Navy fired unceasingly at the Japanese defences, just as they had done the previous day. Then at 0805 hours, as the Navy's guns ceased firing, 72 fighters and bombers attacked the landing beaches for 20 minutes before the naval gunfire was resumed. The marines, wary after Tarawa, had asked for 10 days' bombardment. They got three. As they watched the smoke rise over the island they must surely have thought that was enough. If they did they were wrong, but the navy did give the landing troops a rolling barrage which proved to be very effective as it enabled the assault troops to land against only scattered opposition and to advance inland for about 350yd. It was the first time this technique had been used by the navy.

The landing was a vast and complicated operation. On board the battleship USS *Tennessee* Master Sgt Emmons of the Marine Automatic Weapons Battery watched it swing into action.

'The *Tennessee* was stationed on the left flank of the bombardment line, directly opposite Mt Suribachi, and under 300 yards from the shore line in which position it was our special duty to maintain neutralization of Suribachi. The hundreds of landing craft came up on our port side in a score of boat waves, each some 80 boat 25 yards interval apart, disposed at distances of about 300 yards between waves.

'While the bombardment was at its peak the leading wave of amphibious vehicles had taken station about 200 yards to the seaward

Above left: The invasion fleet approaching Iwo Jima. Mt Suribachi can be seen in the background. *USMC*

Left: Marines of 5th Division moving inland. *USMC*

Below: American dive bombers attacking Japanese positions on Mt Suribachi. *USMC*

of the warships. Behind them the rest of the amphibious vehicles followed by the Higgins boats proceeded to form in parallel lines. In the van was an escort vessel which directed the movement by means of a loud speaker. The speaker blared: "Attention *Tennessee!* You are on the line of departure." The ship at this time was lying broadside to the island, her starboard side engaged. An unofficial voice floated across from our quarter-deck. "What do you expect us to do? Push this big crate sideways?"

'About 0835 the first wave of amphibious vehicles shoved off on their long trip to the beach. The rest of the assault waves followed in lines timed down to the second. Then every ship in the bombardment line increased the tempo of its shelling and bombers dropped load after load of high explosives on enemy prepared positions facing the beach. The noise was incredible. At the same time a dozen gunboats moved in to fire numerous salvoes of rockets into strongpoints at very close range. Then fast planes laid a smokescreen behind the beach to block off the Japs' view. Very soon the shoreline and whole side of Mt Suribachi were completely obscured by flame and smoke.'

The landing was carried out by eight battalions of the 4th and 5th Marine Divisions on beaches on the south-eastern side of the island. On the right hand beaches the 23rd (Col Wensigner) and 25th (Col Lanigan) Regiments of the 4th Division landed on yellow and blue beaches; on the left hand beaches the 27th (Col Wornham) and 28th (Col Liversedge) Regiments of the 5th Division landed on Red and Green beaches. All eight battalions were ashore by 1030 hours and were supported by tanks which came ashore on the last wave of the assault force. Landings continued throughout the day with both divisions putting ashore their reserve regiments, the 4th's 24th (Col Jordan) and the 5th's 26th (Col Graham).

Although the first assault waves met little opposition on the beaches — the enemy either deliberately withholding their fire or being stunned by the rolling barrage — within 15 minutes mortar and artillery fire directed at the beaches began to cause casualties to both divisions. As the morning progressed these casualties began to mount and the crowded beaches were soon strewn with stranded tanks and other vehicles, wrecked landing craft, and with bodies. It was a scene of havoc and destruction that was not to be put straight for some days.

Apart from the enemy's accurate fire, which vanquished all hope that the preliminary bombardment had taken out most of the Japanese defensive positions in the area, the most serious threat to the success of

Above: A landing craft is bracketed by enemy fire while marines of the 5th Division wait to move forward. *USMC*

Left: A marine of the 4th Division engages a Japanese pill box with his tommy gun. This picture was taken three hours after the first wave hit the beach. *USMC*

Bottom left: Two marines inching up on a Japanese pill box on D+1. *USMC*

the landings was the fact that the volcanic sand was much deeper and heavier than had been anticipated, and it bogged down all forms of transportation including the tanks which were urgently needed to support the troops penetrating inland. For a time the 5th Division was critically short of water and ammunition because of this miscalculation but tractors and the use of matting slowly cleared the vital armour and transport off the beaches.

By 1000 hours the enemy were fully alive to the situation and were pouring withering fire on the advancing marines. Cates' 4th Division, facing steep terrain, suffered the most, receiving heavy fire from a ridge on its right flank. 'If I knew the name of the man on the extreme right of the right-hand squad of the right-hand company of 3/25,' said Cates as he watched the landings, 'I'd recommend him for a medal right now.' By the end of the day the division had reached and overrun the southern end of the runway of airfield No 1, but had taken many casualties.

The reason for the uncanny accuracy of the enemy's artillery fire on to the 4th Divisions' beach wasn't discovered until the night of the marines' first day ashore. A marine saw movement in a burnt out Japanese transport on Blue Beach Two. He investigated, and shot a Japanese artillery observer with a radio strapped to his back. The man had been guiding the enemy's fire on to the marine's supply dumps.

The 5th Division also had a hostile reception, with concentrated fire coming from Mt Suribachi. But the ground was more suitable for a rapid advance and it was not long before elements of the 1st Battalion of

Liversedge's 28th Regiment had managed to fight their way across to the west coast of the island. Later that afternoon Liversedge launched an attack against the specific target assigned to him, Mt Suribachi. For this he used his 2nd Battalion while the 1st Battalion mopped up enemy positions which had been bypassed in the quick dash to the west coast. To back his 2nd Battalion he landed his reserve battalion, the 3rd Battalion, commanded by an ex-sergeant, Lt-Col Shephard. Shephard gave his men two objectives when tackling Mt Suribachi:

'1. To secure this lousy piece of real estate so we can get the hell out of it.
'2. To help as many Japs as possible fulfil their oath to die for the Emperor.'

The marines attacked towards the base of the mountain with great determination, but the attack had been delayed and started too late in the day and it soon petered out after about 600yd had been covered. Liversedge then ordered his men to dig in for the night and prepare for a counter-attack. To the right of Liversedge's regiment Wornham's men of the 27th Regiment had pressed inland until they had reached the high ground overlooking the western beaches. Then they struck north until they too met increasingly fierce opposition and dug in for the night.

By the end of the first day the two divisions, with six infantry regiments, six artillery battalions and two tank battalions ashore, held only a narrow beachhead dangerously cluttered with supplies and casualties. They were nowhere near the 0-1 line, the expected limit of advance for the first day. The situation, if not as desperate as Tarawa, was certainly grim. If the Japanese counter-attacked in force there seemed every likelihood that the marines would be driven back into the sea. But it was not part of Kuribayashi's plan to counter-attack in strength. He wanted to preserve his irreplaceable troops and let the Americans do the attacking, and let them batter themselves against what he thought were his impregnable positions. However, limited counter-attacks did take place that first night and subsequently, and infiltration took place throughout the campaign. But there were no *banzai* charges.

Though no major effort was made to dislodge the marines from their beachhead that first night both divisions came under severe mortar and artillery fire. Before Iwo Jima the massive 320mm spigot mortar with its 630lb shell, and the rocket buzz bomb, had been, as someone noted, abstractions in intelligence reports. Now, that first night, they became reality and Cates' men received especially heavy casualties which included the commanding officer of Wensinger's 1st Battalion, who was killed, and the intelligence officer, executive officer and operations officer of Lanigan's 2nd Battalion, who were wounded. Such a heavy toll of officers was to continue throughout the battle, with commands of platoons, companies and even battalions changing with tragic frequency.

At 0830 hours the next morning Liversedge's 2nd and 3rd Battalions resumed their attack towards Mt Suribachi, while his 1st Battalion continued to mop up along the west coast in the regiment's zone. The marines again met heavy fire from concrete blockhouses sited in the scrub and rock near the base of the volcano, and from caves on the sides of the mountain itself. Despite tank support and naval gunfire support the regiment made only 200yd that day, but when the attack was resumed on D+2, with the regiment's 1st Battalion now attacking on the right, better progress was made with the 1st and 3rd Battalions nearing the base of the mountain while the 2nd Battalion filtered men almost right round it. Then the next day, D+3, the encirclement of Mt Suribachi was achieved except for 400yd on the west coast where friendly fire prevented them from making it complete, and on D+4 the attack on the summit was launched by the regiment's 2nd Battalion. Early in the morning a four-man patrol reached the crater and the battalion's commanding officer then called on Lt Schrier to take a 40-man patrol up the south face and hold the crest. 'And put this up on the hill,' he added, giving Schrier the Stars and Stripes.

In full view of the exhausted marines at the base of the mountain, Schrier led the patrol up the steep face of Suribachi, found a piece of pipe, tied the flag to it and hoisted it over the crater. Below, the watching marines started cheering and off the coast the great armada of ships blew whistles and sounded sirens. As the flag was raised two Japanese rushed the patrol. One was shot immediately, the other threw a grenade at the photographer taking a picture of the ceremony. The photographer jumped over the outside edge of the crater and rolled 50ft down the mountain. He smashed his camera but the film was not damaged. Later a larger flag was hoisted over the crater and this ceremony was photographed by Associated Press photographer, Tom Rosenthal. His picture of it was to become one of the most famous photographs of World War 2 and it made Rosenthal famous. Years later he said: 'What difference does it make who took the picture? I took it, but the marines took Iwo Jima.' The Secretary of the Navy, James Forrestal, watched this second flag being raised from where he stood on one of the western beaches of the island. 'This means,' he said, 'a Marine Corps for another 500 years.' Few of those photographed raising these flags, symbols of victory, finished the campaign unscathed and a high percentage of them were killed. For the worst was yet to come.

Over a thousand enemy strongpoints had been encountered during the battle for Suribachi. Some of these had been bypassed, and mopping up took several days. But by D+10 the regiment was ready to rejoin the rest of the landing force in its drive northwards.

While Liversedge was capturing Mt Sur-

Below: Marines of the 4th Division's 24th Regiment moving into the assault along the quarry cliff which overlooked the division's landing beaches. *USMC*

Below right: Marine wiremen advancing at the double. *USMC*

ibachi the rest of the landing force moved inland and along the east coast on a seven battalion front. They met, as they must have expected to, fierce resistance, the Japanese using machine gun, mortar, rocket and artillery fire behind well-laid minefields covered by 47mm anti-tank guns which made the use of tanks extremely hazardous. Despite this resistance Rockey's 5th Division took the rest of airfield No 1 on D+1. On their right the 1st Battalion of Lanigan's 25th Regiment moved beyond it while his 3rd Battalion struck north-east to overrun enemy defences in a quarry cliff that overlooked the 4th Division's beaches. But this proved a costly operation. By 1530 hours K Company had lost three officers, by 1630 hours L Company had lost five, and by 1700 hours I Company had lost six. When L Company eventually reached the top of the quarry the 3rd Battalion's strength was down to 150 men and had to be reinforced with men from Jordan's newly landed 24th Regiment.

The struggle to gain ground on D+2 was just as desperate when at 0810 hours the two divisions resumed their attack to the north-east and west in an all-out effort to reach the 0-1 line which included airfield No 2 and the remains of the village of Motoyama. The advance was preceded by a bombardment of the enemy positions from the air and sea. But this seemed to have little effect for not only were the front line troops continuously fired upon by mortars and artillery but the beaches were too, making the build-up of supplies and the evacuation of the wounded both difficult and costly. To make matters worse the weather, perfect on D-Day, now deteriorated. The 14th Marines lost seven of its 12 howitzers in the heavy surf, firepower that was desperately needed by the hard-pressed men on Cates' 4th Division to whom they were attached.

On the left of the 5th Division's zone Wornham's 27th Regiment, strengthened by a battalion of Graham's 26th Regiment, advanced behind tanks, the more open ground near the west coast making this possible. But they met devastating fire from numerous pillboxes and blockhouses, and from defensive positions in hillside caves. The tanks drew heavy concentrations of mortar fire which caused high casualties amongst the advancing marines, one battalion alone having 62 killed and 212 wounded, and the regiment had only advanced about 1,000yd when it became pinned down.

On the 5th Division's right the 4th Division was also finding the going hard. Casualties were heavy and progress minimal. The Japanese were pouring down heavy mortar and artillery concentrations from the dominating high ground to the north. By the end of D+2, with 40,000 men ashore the

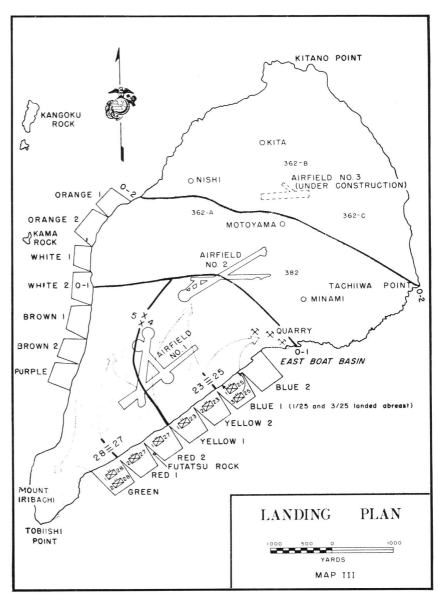

marines had suffered 5,372 casualties, 1,722 of them on D+2 alone, and the corps commander decided that the time had come to commit some of his corps reserve. The 21st Regiment (Col Withers) of the 3rd Marine Division, which had been landed that morning, was therefore sent up to the line to relieve the badly mauled 23rd Regiment, and this it did on D+3 at dawn. Five US Marine Corps correspondents, who later wrote a book *The US Marines on Iwo Jima*, recorded in it:

'The two columns moved quickly across the field, past many mortar and shell holes and piles of wrecked planes. Some of the men glanced at the dark shapes of the green-and-silver planes, thinking of all the bracelets that could be fashioned from the aluminium. But there was no time yet for souvenir-gathering.

'A little before dawn Japanese mortar shells fell on the airfield. The shells whoomped dangerously close to the long,

Above: Map of landing plan. *Reproduced by kind permission of Historical Branch, USMC*

101

snakelike columns; the battalions broke into small groups and quickened their pace. Near the embankment, the 1st Bn twisted around to the right, and the 2nd moved to the left. By the time the two outfits climbed the slope into position before the second airfield, the sky was growing light.

'The survivors of the 23rd were waiting for them. They were bruised, dirty and tired after three sleepless nights and days. They tried to smile. "I was never more happy to see anybody in my life," a machine gunner said to a man relieving him. "I could kiss you."

'The two units changed places, and the bleary-eyed members of the 23rd dragged themselves away. The new arrivals dug into shellholes and looked anxiously around. The odour of death filled the air. The field around and in front them seemed like the surface of the moon. There was hardly a square yard of it unpitted by some kind of shell burst. Dead marines lay in awkward positions among the holes. A red-and-yellow rooster, hit by flying fragments, lay in a pool of blood, between the outspread legs of a dead marine. Volcanic grit particles blew across the barren field, half covering some of the bodies, and piling up in rippled dunes.'

During the night of D+2 Japanese counter-attacks and infiltration were more persistent, the 5th's 27th Regiment on the left of the corps' line coming under especially severe pressure from up to 800 Japanese. The next day it was relieved by Graham's 26th Regiment. Another, smaller group of Japanese were suspected of landing from the sea behind the marines' lines, and on the right of the corps' line the 23rd Regiment, about to be relieved, also came under attack. All these assaults were driven off and although some mopping up had to be done the next morning, at 0835 hours on D+3 the attack was resumed. The fighting in the 5th Division's zone that day was especially bitter and a good deal of hand-to-hand fighting took place. A typical example was when Pfc Maiden of D Company of the 26th's 2nd Battalion was ordered to make contact with the regiment's 3rd Battalion on his right. Crawling up a steep embankment on the edge of No 1 airfield he had just contacted a marine from the 3rd Battalion when they were both rushed by three Japanese who came out of a nearby trench. Both marines opened fire at point-blank range but one Japanese managed to throw a hand grenade before being shot. 'I yelled out to hit the deck,' said Maiden, 'and started tumbling somersault fashion down the steep embankment. I heard the explosion of the grenade and stopped. I looked up and saw the other marine holding his right arm. He had picked up the grenade and had attempted to throw it

Left: Marines of the 5th Division with bazooka and flamethrower advance on D+2. *USMC*

Below left: Dead Japanese were often fitted with booby-traps. This marine is taking no chances as he drags the body out with a sling. *USMC*

Right: The battle at the foot of Mt Suribachi on D+3. *USMC*

Below: Map of Japanese Defence positions.
Reproduced by kind permission of Historical Branch, USMC

NORTHERN

xx 109

SECTOR

RESERVE

3 17
2 26
NLF

145
(-1st Bn)

RESERVE
AREA

2 2
2

EASTERN

MOTOYAMA

310 2

NAVY
314 2
3 26
NLF

WESTERN   SECTOR

311 2

1 26

NLF

309 2

NLF

SOUTHERN

145

SECTOR

SECTOR

MT. SURIBACHI
SECTOR

312 2

MOUNT
SURIBACHI

Main cross-island defenses
Secondary line of defense
Primary defiladed artillery positions
Secondary defiladed artillery positions

1000   0   1000
yards

MAP 1

back at the Japanese, but it had exploded and amputated his right hand at the wrist.'

The corps' line was now coming up against one of the enemy's main defensive lines, a continuous string of mutually defended pillboxes and bunkers, dug-in tanks and concrete emplacements, all interspersed with minefields, that ran along high ground across the width of the island between the two finished airstrips. As a result the advance was again painfully slow and expensive, and that night the marines were repeatedly attacked along the whole of the corps' front, being driven back in places before the assaults were checked.

Towards the end of D+3 the task of evacuating the wounded came near to being impossible. Torrential rain, high surf on the beaches, and the approach of darkness made it impossible to ferry the wounded to the waiting fleet offshore. The crew of LST807 were typical of the courage and initiative shown that night. They volunteered to keep the LST beached throughout the night so that it could be used as an emergency hospital ship. Despite being under constant harassing fire, over 200 casualties were treated aboard overnight. Only two died, a remarkable achievement which showed the ability of the marines and the navy to improvise successfully even in the most adverse circumstances.

When little progress was made on D+4 either, the corps commander decided to continue the drive across the island on a three division front. On D+5, therefore, he landed the balance of Erskine's 3rd Division, less its 3rd Regiment which was kept in reserve, and committed the division in the centre of the line ready for a major assault on No 2 airfield on D+6.

Some progress was made on D+5 however after an extra heavy naval bombardment, which included fire from the battleship USS *Idaho* and the heavy cruiser USS *Pensacola*, and an air strike, was made on the enemy's lines. Three regiments then concentrated their attack on these positions which were denying them No 2 airfield, the 26th Regiment attacking on the left, the 21st Regiment in the centre, and the 24th Regiment on the right. On the right, pushing north towards the east-west runway of No 2 airfield, the 24th Regiment came up against some intricately defended high ground consisting of interlocking enemy fire positions on three main features: Charlie-Dog Ridge, which ran parallel with No 2 airfield's east-west runway on its south side; Hill 382, a craggy outcrop of rocks that dominated the east-west runway and the ground to the south of it; and the amphitheatre, a shallow crescent-shaped basin which was an extension of Charlie-Dog Ridge and dominated by a fortified hill, called Turkey Knob by the marines. Over the next few days of fighting these three features became to be known as 'the Meat Grinder' so horrific were the number of casualties the marines suffered.

In the centre, the 21st Regiment, with strong tank support, kept making attacks across the east-west runway in a desperate effort to get on to the high ground to the north of the runway and subdue the heavy enemy fire coming from it. Eventually two platoons of the 3rd Battalion made it across the strip to the north side and attacked the Japanese with any weapon which came to hand as many rifles and machine guns had become clogged with volcanic ash. Three times they took the high ground and three

times they were driven off, until eventually a concerted attack by both the 21st and 26th Regiments captured it for good. With this one amazingly courageous and determined assault the marines had driven a deep wedge into the enemy's main defences. But elsewhere no headway had been made, and by the end of D+5 the situation was still critical. Something had to be done and the battle-fresh troops of the 3rd Marine Division were the ones who had to do it. At dawn on D+6 Erskine's men took over control of the centre of the corps' line with Col Kenyon's 9th Regiment relieving the 3rd Division's 21st Regiment, which had been landed ahead of the rest of the division, and was by now battle-weary and suffering from high casualties.

The 3rd Division's first task was to cross the airfield's main runway and clear the high ground to the north of it. But both runways gave the enemy a perfect field of fire and nine marine tanks were knocked out while trying to get across. On either side of the 3rd Division the 4th and 5th Divisions were also pinned down and were taking heavy losses, and by the end of D+6 the combat efficiency of Cates's 4th Division on the right of the line was down to 55%.

For the next three days the landing force struggled to move forward but it was not until the end of D+8 that Kenyon's 9th Regiment finally succeeded in capturing the high ground to the north of No 2 airfield, which included the strategically placed Hill 199-0 and Hill Peter. The regiment was then relieved by the 21st Regiment, which on D+9 continued to push north on a two-battalion front. It was here that the marines encountered one especially bizarre form of defence when elements of one company were

Above: Marines of the 5th Division hunting out snipers at the southern end of Iwo Jima. *USMC*

Above left: A marine from E Coy, 9th Marines charges forward with flamethrower during the fighting for No 2 airfield. *USMC*

Above right: 4.5in rocket trucks in action on D+4. *USMC*

Above, far right: A Japanese hillside fortification. *USMC*

Right: Blasting an enemy position with flamethrowers. They were the only weapons which forced the Japanese into the open. *USMC*

Top: Marines of L Coy, 3rd Battalion, 21st Marines, moving forward under heavy mortar and machine gun fire in an attempt to take No 2 airfield on D+5 having just relieved marines from 4th Division. *USMC*

Above: Marines of the 5th Division in the front line, D+8. *USMC*

approaching what appeared to be huge mounds of earth. As they got closer these mounds began to move, rocks and shrubbery falling away to reveal five Japanese tanks which rose up out of the ground and moved on the startled marines. For a moment it looked as if the whole of the battalion's left flank was in danger of collapsing but bazookas and flamethrowers were rushed forward and three of the tanks were destroyed. The other two withdrew but were later destroyed by an air strike.

On the right of the 21st Regiment's zone of operation the regiment's 3rd Battalion now managed to advance rapidly, and by the afternoon of D+9 had captured the remains of the village of Motoyama and the high

ground which overlooked the uncompleted No 3 airfield. On its left flank however the regiment's 1st Battalion met heavy opposition and the delay in its advance opened a gap between its right flank and the left flank of the 3rd Battalion, so the regiment's 2nd Battalion was sent forward to attack through it, bypass the enemy holding up the 1st Battalion and regain contact with the 3rd Battalion. After heavy fighting this was achieved and an uneven but continuous line was made for the night. The 3rd Division had, at last, breached the enemy's main defensive line and was poised to strike rapidly north-east to the coast and so divide the Japanese garrison.

For the next three days the regimental commander of the 21st Regiment, Col Withers, pressed home his attack through the gap he had opened in the Japanese defences and overran the third airfield, though the Japanese still occupied the surrounding high ground and were able to sweep the runways with gunfire. Enemy strongpoints on Hill 362B to the north now prevented Withers from advancing to the coast. Although this hill was in the 5th Division's zone of operation permission was granted for the 3rd Division to clear it and on D+11 (2 March) an assault was launched. But despite a rolling barrage and destroyer gunfire support neither regiments involved in the attack could make any headway, coming under fire from concealed artillery pieces and hostile flanking fire from high ground to their left. On their right a concealed artillery gun which could not be located also caused heavy casualties. The next day the 5th Division resumed responsibility for the hill's capture and managed to overrun it, enabling the 3rd Division to resume its advance. The 2nd Battalion of the division's 21st Regiment now gained the peak of the one remaining defended feature before the coast, Hill 357, on D+13, but on the division's right flank

Col Kenyon's 9th Regiment was being held up by strong defensive positions in the area of Hills 331 and 362-C. When it became apparent that these were now the enemy's last main positions in the division's zone Col Withers turned south-east to help Col Kenyon's men envelop them. But by the end of D+13 the attack had ground to a halt after meeting fierce resistance.

While the 3rd Division was advancing up the centre of the island and overrunning the airfields, the 5th Division was encountering increasingly difficult terrain and fierce opposition from a well entrenched and fanatical enemy. Having waited on D+6 for the 3rd Division to move forward the 5th Division continued the attack on D+7. The Japanese main line of defence — which the other two divisions had found so hard to crack — was now in front of it, the core of this line in the division's zone being an intricate system of blockhouses, pillboxes and natural caves on a hill designated 362-A. It was riddled with underground tunnels and though only 362ft high the terrain of this rabbit-warren was rugged, the northern side having a sheer cliff some 80ft high while the southern side was devoid of any vegetation being just a jumble of rocks and crevices.

For two days the division fought desperately to break through the Japanese line of defences and with equal tenacity the Japanese clung to them. Earlier in the campaign the enemy had retreated when out-numbered or out-manoeuvred but now they stayed where they were until they were burnt out of their positions, or killed, or buried alive by high explosive charges. Those who tried to make a dash for the open were shot down. Each strongpoint had to be reduced one by one but by noon on D+9 the 3rd Battalion of the division's 27th Regiment had reached the foot of Hill 362-A and that afternoon a patrol from the battalion's I Company started for the top. It managed to get there but then dropped back for the night and a fierce counter-attack by about 100 Japanese was later repulsed only after bitter hand-to-hand fighting and severe marine casualties.

On D+10 the 28th Regiment, having disposed of Mt Suribachi, relieved the 27th Regiment, and, with the 3rd Battalion of Col Graham's 26th Regiment attached, took over the attack, and by 1030 hours the crest of Hill 362-A was again in the hands of the marines. But this did not end the matter as it was then found that the Japanese had placed strongpoints on the reverse slope, and these caused heavy casualties. But the whole hill was eventually cleared and the division advanced to clear Nishi Ridge to the north and Hill 362-B to the east.

With the taking of 362-A the enemy's main defence line had now been breached in the 5th Division's zone of operation but, unlike the 3rd Division, a rapid advance beyond it was not found to be possible as the

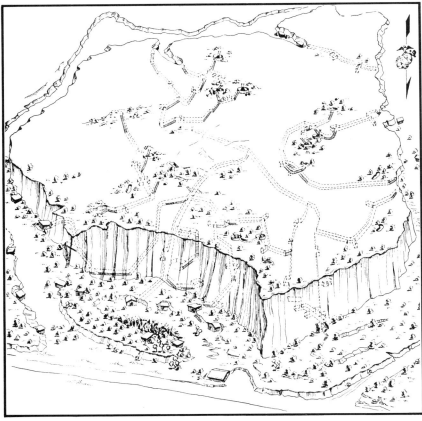

Below left: A wounded marine is helped to safety. *USMC*

Below: Sketch of Hill 362A prepared by 31st US Naval Construction Battalion.

enemy was defending the whole area in depth. To make matters worse the terrain was now so rocky and broken that tanks often could not operate. Armoured bulldozer tanks were therefore used to clear a path to the target under attack which enabled a tank to move forward and engage it. This became part of a novel method of warfare perfected by the marines. The tank action report commented:

'The three-tank platoon proved particularly effective at this time. The terrain was of such a nature that the infantry would not always protect the tanks from suicide attack. Thus the tanks had to protect themselves. The tactics involved were as follows: the leading tank would do the fighting, the next tank would cover the right and the last tank the left. When the resistance was overcome the dozer tank would come in and doze paths to all the caves, pillboxes and other emplacements. The dozer would withdraw and then the flame tank would move in and burn the area. The method was always successful. The Japs at this time kept close contact with our own front lines and thus nullified the effect of our artillery. Thus it was the only way that our forces could advance using the task force mentioned: a platoon of tanks accompanied by a flame tank and dozer.'

Using this effective but laborious method of advancing, the division slowly pushed forward until by D+12 (3 March) it held a line north of Nishi and across the crest of Hill 362-B which had been so troublesome to Erskine's 3rd Division. But hits were only achieved after fierce fighting in conditions well described later by the division's Intelligence Officer who wrote in his D-2 Operation Report that . . .

'in the final defensive area north of Nishi the increased natural defensive strength of the ground and its subterranean defensive features compensated for the reduced amounts of concrete and steel used by the Japs . . . Volcanic eruption has littered the whole northern end of the island with outcrops of sandstone and loose rock. The sandstone outcrops made digging easy for the Japs . . . Our troops obtained cover only by defilade or by piling loose rocks on the surface to form rock-reveted positions. A series of irregularly eroded, crisscrossed gorges with precipitous sides resulted in a series of compartments of various shapes. These were usually small but some extended for several hundred yards. The compartments were lined with a labrynth (sic) of natural and artificial caves which covered the approaches from all directions. Fields of fire were usually limited to twenty-five yards, and a unique or at least unusual characteristic of the Japanese defensive positions in that area

was that the reverse slopes were as strongly fortified as were the forward slopes.'

On the division's eastern flank two companies of Col Graham's 26th Regiment's 2nd Battalion led the fight to take the rest of Hill 362-B. The assault was short, sharp and bloody and the men used rocket launchers, flamethrowers, and demolitions to winkle the enemy out of the dense network of interconnecting caves and pillboxes that covered the southern and western slopes. Both company commanders became casualties in this bitter fighting, and on this day alone the 5th Division won five Medals of Honor, three of them posthumously. One who survived to receive his decoration was Sgt Harrell who, on dawn watch by Nishi Ridge, repelled single-handedly a determined Japanese attack on his post. During the attack his thigh was broken by a grenade and his left hand was blown off. With his right hand he then shot one Japanese and when others rushed forward Harrell fought them off until eventually another grenade blew off his other hand. At dawn he was found with five dead Japs around him. But his post had not been taken.

The next day brought little change to the overall situation and on 5 March, in common with the rest of the corps, the division spent the day reorganising. This was the day that the 1st Platoon of B Company 28/1 got its fourth commanding officer. The first had been wounded and evacuated five days previously; the second, a sergeant, was killed the same day; the third, also a sergeant, took over until an officer could be found to take command. When he arrived he only lasted four days. Altogether this particular platoon was to have seven commanders.

As the men of the 5th Division slowly chipped their way through the enemy's defensive line the 4th Division on the other end of the corps' line was meeting the fiercest fighting of all. By D+6, as has been noted, its operational efficiency was down to 55% and it was still trying to overcome the huge enemy network of fortified positions centred on Hill 382, Charlie-Dog Ridge and the amphitheatre. The Turkey Knob which dominated the last was not very high but it had had built into it a three-tiered reinforced concrete blockhouse. It was to prove to be one of the strongest defences on the island. Its domination of the amphitheatre — itself a vast booby trap of prepared enemy positions — was to cause severe casualties when the 4th Division attacked on D+7 on a five-battalion front. On the left flank Col Wensinger's 23rd Regiment pressed forward towards Hill 382 and by late afternoon had captured its south-west slopes but later had to withdraw. In the centre of the division's

front Col Lanigan's 25th Regiment could not break through or subdue the enemy's strong positions around Turkey Knob. That night both regiments were subjected to harassing fire from mortars and artillery, and the enemy tried, unsuccessfully, to infiltrate the regiment's lines. Hand-to-hand fighting went on throughout the hours of darkness.

The next day, D+8, the attack on Hill 382 and on Turkey Knob continued. Despite the many casualties being caused by enemy tanks buried up to their turrets in crevices, at one point men of the 23rd Regiment's 3rd Battalion had nearly reached Hill 382's summit, and were fighting for the wrecked radar station on top of it, when orders were received to withdraw for the night to better defensive positions. At the end of that day Turkey Knob, too, was still in the enemy's hands and no ground had been gained.

For five more days the 4th Division hammered away at 'the Meat Grinder' in some of the fiercest fighting seen on Iwo Jima. No sooner had one pillbox on Hill 382 been overcome, for instance, than the enemy infiltrated back into it by means of underground passages. Turkey Knob proved equally difficult to take and though at one point a 75mm pack howitzer was dismantled and then miraculously manhandled up the steep and rocky terrain to a position where it could pour direct fire into the blockhouse, the Japanese kept firing back. In the end, however, fire from the blockhouse was neutralised and the exhausted marines, their morale raised by the appearance of the howitzer amongst them, managed to advance the 75yd needed for them to storm the blockhouse the next day. Then, on 3 March, Hill 382 was not only taken but made secure at night, though the toll in taking it had been a terrible one in the number of men wounded or killed. When the battle was over E Company of the 24th Regiment's 2nd Battalion, one of the two companies to take part in the final assault, was so depleted it had to be merged with another company. Earlier, one platoon, which had managed to reach the top, had been cut off. One eye-witness said: 'We put down a smoke-screen to get these men out. Japanese fire was cutting them down mercilessly. Ten wounded men had to be left behind. One marine, his leg broken, lay for 36 hours on the side of the hill, a dead buddy beside him. When our troops regained the hill he was rescued. Our tanks simply could not operate on these rocky hillsides. On the pushoff they tried it and two of them struck mines. Two others were knocked out by direct fire from anti-tank guns. We finally took Hill 382 the hard way, sending men in a frontal assault against the Japanese, who had been ordered to defend their positions to the death.'

Pockets of resistance still remained in the amphitheatre, but by 5 March, the day of reorganisation, Maj-Gen Cates could justifiably feel that he had finally penetrated the enemy's main defensive line in his zone of operation. The combat efficiency of his division was now down to the dangerously low level of 45% but not only had he broken through but, even more important, his division's capture of Hill 382 and the Turkey Knob now denied the Japanese essential artillery observation posts, and from that time the effectiveness of the enemy's mortar and artillery fire on the marines' rear bases was limited.

Two-thirds of Iwo Jima was now in the hands of the marines, but the remaining third, ringed by the enemy's secondary defen-sive line, was some of the most rugged on the island. It was this part that contained the most active sulphur holes and fissures, and where it was impossible to live in foxholes because of the heat. Additionally, the smell of erupting sulphur and the stench of the dead made the island a veritable hell hole.

Both the finished airfields were now operational and on 6 March Brig-Gen Moore of the US Army took up his duties as air defence commander. One of the objectives in taking Iwo Jima had therefore been achieved. But the other, to destroy the Japanese forces on the island, was to take another two weeks of bitter fighting.

The attack on this last third of the island was launched at 0800 hours on 6 March after an intense bombardment by corps and divisional artillery, and naval shelling. Again the fighting was fierce and the ground gained minimal. On the left flank the 5th Division had to contend with concentrated rifle, machine gun and mortar fire, and with phosphorous shells, as they tried to advance north from the reverse slopes of Hill 362-B. Each pillbox, bunker and cave had to be taken out one by one, the enemy in them destroyed and the positions sealed by engineers with explosives to prevent reinfiltration. The rugged terrain made close tank support impossible and artillery fire largely ineffective, but the next day gains were made against enemy positions in the area of Nishi village by the 27th Regiment, while in the centre of the division's zone of action the 26th Regiment launched a successful pre-dawn surprise attack to overrun a strong pocket of resistance. With this pocket cleared H Company of the Regiment's 3rd Battalion then spearheaded the advance and came upon what was obviously a major enemy command post. A firefight developed but eventually the Japanese resistance petered out and it appeared as if they had been cleared from the numerous caves and tunnels that riddled the ridge, and the marines warily climbed on to its crest.

'Suddenly the earth began to tremble. The scarred hill quivered violently in a rising crescendo ending in an explosion which could be heard all over Iwo Jima. The entire ridge and the marines on it were blown high into the air. Men nearby were stunned by the concussion ... the ridge was a mass of twisted, torn, burning rock and sand. Smoke rose from a ragged hole so large that a good-sized apartment house could have been slipped inside.' The Japanese in the command post had blown themselves — and 43 marines — sky-high; a typical example of the fanatical way the Japanese defended the island.

Meanwhile, in the centre of the corps' line Erskine's 3rd Division ran up against what its War Diary described as 'a fortress-like organisation likened only to that encountered in WW1 or in the fortified sectors of the present European war'; while on the eastern side of the island the 4th Division, having overcome the enemy's resistance on Hill 382 and Turkey Knob, just ran up against yet another series of defended ridges.

As it was by now obvious that the intensive artillery and naval barrages which preceded the corps' attacks had been almost totally ineffective, Maj-Gen Erskine decided to make a surprise night attack on his division's next main objective, Hill 362C. At 0500 hours on 7 March Withers' 21st Regiments, with the 3rd Battalion of the 9th Regiment attached, attacked south-east on the left of the division's zone, and the balance of the 9th Regiment on the right side of the zone. The attack completely surprised the enemy but unfortunately the line of departure had been miscalculated so that when 3rd Battalion 9/3 thought they were capturing Hill 362-C they were in fact on the smaller Hill 331. Nevertheless, after heavy opposition from a now thoroughly awakened enemy, Hill 362-C was taken by late afternoon. Later the commanding officer of the 3rd Battalion commented that, 'although nearly all the basic dope was inaccurate (information from maps, etc) the strategy proved very sound, since it turned out that the open ground taken under cover of darkness was the most heavily fortified of all the terrain captured that day, in fact the strongest center of resistance encountered from Motoyama village to the beach.'

The 9th Regiment attacking east towards the same hill had less success though initially both the 2nd Battalion, commanded by Lt-Col Cushman, and the 1st Battalion commanded by Maj Glass, managed to advance

Above left: A Marine combat photographer takes a shot of a burning Sherman tank hit by Japanese artillery. *USMC*

Left: Stretcher bearers race forward past a dead Japanese. *USMC*

Above: Dead Japanese with light machine gun. *USMC*

some 200yd or more. However, they were then cut off from the rear and isolated. A pincer movement was started from the north and south by parts of the 21st and 23rd Regiments in an attempt to trap the enemy in front of Cushman's battalion. But two of Cushman's companies were cut to pieces and by the time they were rescued — after Hill 362-C was taken — only 19 remained of F Company and eight of E Company. Even when Hill 362-C was taken the Japanese continued to fight fiercely despite being surrounded. The area in which they were contained became known as 'Cushman's Pocket'.

Two days after overrunning Hill 362-C a six-man patrol from the 21st Regiment reached the beach of the north-east shore, and sent back to the corps commander a water bottle of sea water marked 'For inspection, not consumption!' to show that the vital breakthrough had been made. The Japanese garrison was now split in two.

This achieved, the 21st Regiment began moving north-west towards Kitano Pt in support of the 5th Division, and the 9th Regiment swung south-east to support the 4th Division, which still had a fight on its hands with the last organised pocket of enemy resistance around Tachiwa Pt. Also, Cushman's Pocket still had to be reduced, but this took many days and it was not until 16 March that men from the 3rd Division eventually eliminated the last Japanese in that area. Cushman said:

'We beat against this position for eight con-tinuous days, using every supporting weapon. When relieved, we had destroyed all anti-tank fire in our zone of action and had eliminated 250 yards of the resistance. The core — the main objective of the sector — still remained. The battalion was exhausted. Almost all leaders were gone and the battalion numbered about 400, including 350 replacements.

'It is evident that the first phase [the battle for airfield No 2] had taken the skilled leaders and the "drive" out of the battalion. The second phase was a continuous pillbox assault for the infantry, and we lacked the skilled troops. Supporting weapons were superb again and accounted for our limited gains — some four hundred yards in eight days.

'The enemy position was a maze of caves, pillboxes, emplaced tanks, stone walls and trenches. Only those immediately in front of the troops could be located and, because the Japs used smokeless powder, some of them were not known. Out of about 150 of these positions (by later count), we knew roughly twenty or thirty of them.'

On the left of the 3rd Division — as Erskine's men were struggling to take Hill 362-C — the 5th Division made important progress by reaching high ground dominating the north coast of the island. But the 4th Division on the right were again pinned down despite heavy air strikes against the enemy's positions. Then on the night of 8/9 March the division had to repel the heaviest counter-attack the enemy had so far launched on the island. Captured documents later revealed that the Japanese had planned to infiltrate the marines' lines and make for airfield No 1 where planes and installations were to be destroyed. This night attack was successfully repulsed with the aid of an artillery barrage and the next morning the bodies of 784 Japanese were counted. This abortive raid weakened the enemy considerably and that day the division was able to advance rapidly against only light opposition, and at 1500 hours a patrol reached the coast on the division's left flank.

The enemy in the 4th Division's zone was now surrounded in a pocket around Tachiwa Pt and on 12 March General Cates sent a message to the trapped Japanese's brigade commander and also broadcast it in Japanese by loudspeaker:

'This is the Commanding General of the 4th Division, US Marines, making a direct appeal to the Brigade Commander and his command to honorably surrender. You have fought a gallant and heroic fight, but you must have realised that the island of Iwo Jima has been lost to you. You can gain nothing by further resistance, nor is there any reason to die when you can honorably surrender and live to render valuable service to your country in the future. I promise and guarantee you and the members of your staff the best of treatment. I respectfully request you accept my terms of honorable surrender. I again appeal to you in the name of humanity — surrender without delay.'

The appeal was ignored and, well dug in and secreted in deep caves and tunnels, the Japanese continued to fight hard and skilfully. It took five more days of hard fighting to clear the area but on 16 March (D+25), after 60 Japanese had made a last desperate break for freedom, Cates was able to report that the last of the enemy in his zone of operation had been eliminated.

On the opposite side of Iwo Jima, on the same day, 9 March, that the six-man patrol from the 4th Division reached the sea, the 28th Regiment of the 5th Division ran into heavy enemy fire from a ridge running southwest from Kitano Pt. It soon became apparent that the enemy was now preparing a final stand in this area for there was much activity on the 5th Division's front that night and the next night with smoke being used to conceal the movement of troops and supplies into the pocket. This last defensive position was almost certainly under the direct command of Lt-Gen Kuribayashi himself, though this will never be known for certain as his body was never found.

On the night of 11/12 March the Japanese managed to infiltrate the division's lines — one Japanese was wearing a marine uniform and carrying an M1 American rifle, a deception the enemy used frequently on Iwo Jima — but were driven off. The next day bitter resistance was met again with the marines facing a heavily defended rocky gorge covered by supporting fire from the ridge which had been holding up the regiment's advance for days. But on D+22 the 27th

Regiment at last managed to break through on the 28th's right in its drive towards Kitano Pt, while the 21st Regiment advanced up to the beaches on the eastern coast. The Japanese again infiltrated the division's lines that night (12/13 March), but when morning came the 27th Regiment made further gains before being relieved — the regiment being by this time, as the divisional history put it, either 'dead or dead tired' — and the next day the 21st Regiment reached Kitano Pt. Iwo Jima was very nearly, but not quite, in American hands, and on 16 March (D+25), after the pocket of resistance around Tachiwa Pt fell to the 4th Division, the corps commander declared that all Japanese resistance had ceased.

But the 5th Division still had another 10 days hard fighting in front of them before Gen Schmidt's announcement could be said to be true, for the 26th and 28th Regiments now came right up against the last formidable enemy pocket, the place where Kuribayashi had decided to make his final stand, a rocky gorge which soon became known to the marines as 'Death Valley' or 'Bloody Gorge'. The gorge was only between 200 and 500yd wide, and 700yd long, but it contained within it several jagged rocky outcrops which were major obstacles in themselves. The whole gorge was strewn with boulders and pock-marked with caves. Each strongpoint had to be taken individually and a path to each prepared by armoured bulldozers before the supporting flamethrower tanks could manoeuvre into position to burn out the enemy.

One of the officers given the task of clearing 'Bloody Gorge' was Lt Barrett of the 26th's 1st Battalion. During the fighting on Iwo Jima, Barrett's company, B, had become so depleted that it was now amalgamated with A Company for this final push against the Japanese. This combined unit had Barrett as its Executive Officer. He wrote afterwards:

Below: Marines waiting to attack No 3 airfield. *USMC*
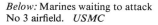

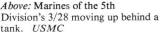
Above: Marines of the 5th Division's 3/28 moving up behind a tank. *USMC*

Above right: Marines flushing out snipers from the honeycomb ridges which were a feature of the northern part of Iwo. *USMC*

'Getting into the line late Sunday afternoon was a harrowing and deathly experience; I wanted the company set up for the night on a slight ridge perhaps 25/30 yards ahead, and said to Hutchins, one of my few remaining platoon sergeants, "Take your men down there, Hutch, and dig in for the night." "Jesus Christ, Lieutenant, why is it always my platoon?" "You and Blackman are all we have left," I explained to him, "and he's over there on the right. I just want you to tie in on his left." "Okay, but..." W-R-A-C-K! A rifle shot came from our left. Hutch fell dead, shot squarely between the eyes. His great black boots protruded ominously from beneath the poncho we threw over him. Hutch stood only about four feet from me when he was hit.

'The next morning was even worse. 1st-Sgt John Farris and I were huddled in our foxhole determining the number of men left to us when the lethal sniper fired again. Farris fell forward with a bullet through his chest. The same round clipped a marine behind Farris. Not for the first time a Japanese marksman had nailed two of our men with one shot. We carried the wounded back to the aid station and started through Death Valley. We didn't get far. Even our battalion commander, Colonel Pollock, was hit and one after another our valiant men fell.'

It is worth recording that when B Company left Iwo Jima only 32 out of the original 246 men climbed aboard the troopship — and many of these had been wounded and had returned to duty.

By the evening of 24 March (D+33) the 28th Regiment had confined the enemy to an area 50yd square, and this was overrun the following morning. Organised resistance was at last at an end on the island. In other areas however there was still sporadic fighting by isolated groups of Japanese and in the early hours of 26 March some 200 or 300 Japanese attacked rear echelon troops and caused a good deal of confusion, and a number of casualties, before they were eliminated. About 40 of this party carried swords which showed a high proportion of them were officers or NCOs. One of their number was captured alive and he said the group had been led by Kuribayashi himself, but no proof of this could be found. On the same day as this attack occurred operational command of the island was handed over to the US Army garrison.

Capturing Iwo Jima had been expected to take 14 days. It took 36, and over a third of the entire marine force — 5,931 dead, 17,372 wounded — had become casualties. But the marines had won their most famous battle yet. They will always be remembered for Iwo Jima.

115

Buffaloes assembled on the banks of the Elbe. *IWM*

The Five Rivers Campaign

In January 1945, with the war in Europe at a critical stage and with the British Army desperately short of troops for the advance into Germany, the 1st Special Services Brigade, now renamed the 1st Commando Brigade, was sent to Holland to take part in the task of rolling back the German Army in North-West Europe. The brigade consisted of two Army Commandos and two Royal Marine Commandos, Nos 45 and 46.

Between the northern flank of the Allied front line and the Baltic ports, which was the brigade's ultimate destination, lay one Dutch and four German rivers: the Maas, the Rhine, the Weser, the Aller, and the Elbe. On each occasion when these rivers had to be crossed the brigade was given the task of supplying the troops to either create or enlarge a beachhead.

So it happened that the marines, even when fighting many miles from sea, retained their amphibious role by moving into action by waterborne assaults.

Top: Embarking for the crossing of the River Maas. *RM Archives*

Above: Approaching the enemy held east bank of the River Maas. *RM Archives*

Linne on the east bank in the US Ninth Army's sector to protect the left flank of the British 7th Armoured Division moving north-east.

The operation was carried out by 45Cdo and 6Cdo, with 3Cdo in reserve. A squadron of the Royal Tank Regiment was under the brigade's command for the operation. As snow lay thickly on the ground (the area was later called 'the ice box' by those who were there), these tanks were mostly painted white or had white camouflage. The temperature was well below zero. 'My recollection of that battle,' said Bryan Samain who was 45Cdo's Intelligence Officer at the time, 'was the bitter cold, the snow, the blanketing whiteness of the countryside, and that, yet again, the brigade had bumped into a particular SS unit, Battlegroup Hubner, who were courageous fighters.'

The attack began at 0830 hours on 23 January, and Maasbracht and Brachterbeek were entered unopposed. A Troop moved through Brachterbeek and on towards the railway station south-east of Linne. When the leading section reached a row of houses on the outskirts of a small village called St Joostbrug it came under small arms fire. The section, led by Lt Thomas, rushed the German positions under cover of extremely accurate support fire from Marine Patrick's Bren gun and cleared them, but could then move no further. The section behind then came under machine gun fire from the left flank but managed to reach the safety of the houses, but when the third section, led by Lt Cory, tried to join the other two sections, there were several casualties and it remained pinned down. The rest of the Commando, which was still in Brachterbeek, then started being shelled and mortared. Attempts were made to extricate A Troop under cover of smoke but the weight of the enemy's fire made this impossible.

At this point, A Troop's medical orderly, Lance-corporal Harden RAMC, heard that Lt Cory and two others had been wounded and were lying in the open. Despite having to cross 120yd of ground exposed to the enemy's fire, Harden ran from cover and tended to the three wounded men. He then returned carrying one of the wounded with him and it was noticed that not only were there bullet holes in his uniform but that he had been slightly wounded in the side. His troop commander told him not to go out again and that he would arrange for tanks to rescue the other two men. Harden, however, insisted that the men would not survive much longer in the intense cold, and while tank support was being arranged, he and two volunteers went out with a stretcher and brought back another of the wounded. Harden then returned a third time and, with

After several months of reorganisation and training in England, 45(RM)Cdo and 46(RM)Cdo, now commanded by two brothers, Lt Col W. N. Gray and Lt Col T. M. Gray, returned to the Continent to fight with the Allied forces in North-Western Europe as members of the 1st Commando Brigade.

But before the brigade could enter Germany the enemy had to be cleared from the River Maas north and south of the town of Venlo in south-west Holland. 45Cdo's first encounter in this campaign came when the brigade (less 46Cdo which was temporarily posted to Antwerp) was called upon to create a bridgehead across the Maas by capturing the villages of Maasbracht, Brachterbeek and

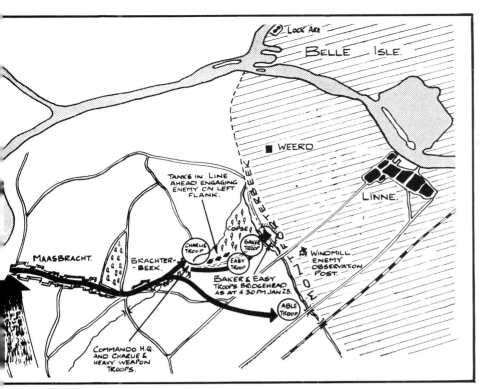

Above: Map of 45Cdo's action at Brachterbeek.
Reproduced from Commando Men, *by kind permission Bryan Samain*

only to cross the marsh but the stream too and get into a gulley the other side which they soon cleared. B Troop's commander, hearing the sound of battle, hurried his troop forward to support Riley and the gulley was soon firmly in the hands of the marines with D Troop later coming up to reinforce the position. By the time darkness came an all-round defensive position had been taken up in the gulley while further to the east A Troop were at last able to extricate themselves from St Joostbrug.

The night, however, was not to pass peacefully for at 2130 hours B Troop's commander, Capt Day, was told noises could be heard beyond the marines' perimeter. 'The Troop stood-to,' said Captain Day, 'and every man was waiting for my order to open fire. When the Hun was within certain killing distance B Troop opened fire with all available machine guns and tommy guns — even with the Troop PIAT. One or two white-clad Huns ran away. The remainder stayed very still. I then brought down our own artillery fire on to our own positions as we would be in slit trenches while the Germans infiltrating into the gulley to our right would be in the open.' This tactic was successful as several more Germans were killed by the shells while only one marine was wounded.

With the bridgehead still intact the next morning, the marines were relieved by an army Commando who made short work of the rest of the German line, and by the morning after the brigade had occupied Linne without further fighting. Intermittent fighting did continue in the area however for some time and included an attempt by 45Cdo to clear a German-held island on the Maas, and it was not until the beginning of March that intensive training began with amphibious vehicles for the crossing of the Rhine. The brigade's task for this operation was to create a bridgehead on the east bank and then to help seize the town of Wesel, the most important centre of communications in the area. The plan was for the landing to be made at night in a low-lying basin of barren marshy ground called Grav Insel, about two miles downstream from Wesel. As high ground dominated this area it was essential to be away from it before daylight, and it was therefore decided that the marines would be only lightly equipped.

The landings were preceded by a savage artillery bombardment on the German positions in the area of Grav Insel, and preceded and followed by bombing raids on Wesel itself. The artillery bombardment was carried out on the brigade's front by no less than three super-heavy batteries, one heavy regiment, seven medium regiments, ten field regiments, one HAA Regiment, one 3.7 mountain regiment, and innumerable mortar

the same volunteers, brought back Lt Cory. With about 50yd to go to safety Harden was hit in the head and died instantly.

A Troop's sergeant-major, who witnessed Harden's courageous actions said later that Harden had said to him, '. . . that the casualties must be got in from the extreme cold to have a chance to survive. During my conversations with him, he gave no thought to his own safety provided the wounded could be got in, and was cool and calm in dealing with his patients even though he had himself been hit on one of his journeys.' For, as his citation put it, 'the magnificent example he set of cool courage and determination', Harden was posthumously awarded the Victoria Cross.

The CO now decided to try and outflank the German line which ran along the far side of a stream called the Montforterbeek. He therefore ordered E Troop, followed by B Troop to move along the line of an embankment east of Brachterbeek and try and break through the enemy's position. Tanks were then sent up to support the two troops. All went well until E Troop's leading section reached a small copse where it came under heavy fire from an enemy position further along the embankment. Several casualties were suffered and the troop's advance held up. B Troop's commander now decided to probe the left flank and sent forward one section, led by Lt Riley, to see whether it was possible to cross some frozen marshland in order to attack the enemy's positions along the Montforterbeek. The section soon made contact with the enemy and managed not

Left: 3in mortar team in action, Lower Maas, Holland.
RM Archives

Right: Moving up along the banks of the River Maas. *RM Archives*

teams. 'Never in the history of human warfare have so many guns supported so few men,' the brigade commander told the marines before they crossed. 'When you go in tonight, cut the hell out of them.'

The first wave of Buffaloes (LVTs) carrying B Troop of 45Cdo and one section of Y Troop, entered the Rhine at 2200 hours on 23 March. B Troop's mission was to capture a farmhouse about 400yd from the river in the grounds of which two 88mm guns were positioned, while the section from Y Troop was to dispose of any Germans still manning trenches in the immediate vicinity of the beachhead. In fact, the section had little difficulty in clearing the German trenches as the artillery barrage had been so intense they soon collected over 60 very dazed prisoners.

B Troop, however, encountered greater resistance. One of its Buffaloes carrying a sub-section and the FOB had been hit during the crossing. This reduced the troop's number to about 40, and without the FOB the troop commander, Capt Gibbon, was without any means of calling for direct artillery support. Nevertheless, he pressed home his attack on the farmhouse by closely following a prearranged rolling barrage from the other shore, and achieved almost complete surprise. 'We followed the barrage in two lines,' said Capt Gibbon, who was later awarded the MC for his part in the operation, 'keeping as far as possible within 25 yards of it. It was dark and very noisy and difficult to judge the exact distance from the moving barrage of bursting shells. The object was to keep close to the barrage so that when we got to the German positions we would be amongst them before they could man their positions.'

The two 88mm guns were quickly overrun and rendered harmless, and the farmhouse was surrounded. Most of the Germans had hidden in a cellar but there was some brief hand-to-hand fighting as the marines broke into the farmhouse itself, and Marine Hazell, for one, had to use his Tommy gun as a club. 60 prisoners were taken.

This rapid progress had gained valuable ground but Capt Gibbon had no means of communicating with the artillery to tell them where his troop was located, and it soon became evident that one section had gone too far forward and was in danger from it. Marine Hazell was therefore ordered to bring the section back and he immediately ran through a salvo that burst all around him. On returning with the section it was found that two men were missing and Hazell immediately went forward again through the barrage of shell fire, located the men and brought them back to safety. For this act of bravery, Marine Hazell was awarded the Military Medal.

Within quarter of an hour of B Troop landing at Grav Insel the balance of the Commando was ashore without incident and had reinforced the bridgehead. A and Z Troops then moved to the right and took their first objective, another farmhouse situated about 1,000yd from the landing beach before moving on and overrunning some nearby anti-aircraft posts. 45Cdo's turn to cross the Rhine came just as 250 Lancaster bombers of the RAF started their second raid on Wesel, a raid which has gone down in the history book as the closest support bombing of the war. 'The sight was almost beyond description,' wrote an eyewitness. 'To our right Wesel was being annihilated; to our front we could see the angry red glow of the supporting barrage; to the left one buffalo on the far side was ablaze; overhead we could hear the rushing wind of the long-range shells, and at short intervals the bark of bofors guns firing tracers to mark the flanks.'

The route into Wesel was now marked by white tape, a technique developed by the brigade commander, Brig Mills-Roberts. It involved a small detail of men unwinding a reel of white tape while moving forward with the leading section of a troop which probed forward at night to the brigade's objective along a previously planned route carefully plotted to avoid enemy positions. '1,200 men quietly slipping through in single file sounds unbelievable,' commented one troop commander from 46Cdo, 'but we did precisely that on all the rivers and each time with complete success. When daylight came the enemy found an entire brigade drawn up in fighting formation in his rear. Not only was this successful in the sense of beating the enemy — but it also kept our own casualties to a bare minimum compared with what they could have been in a frontal attack.'

Once in Wesel — 'moving through the town was like entering Dante's Inferno, and around us we could could see blazing shells that had once been houses and shops' — both Commandos headed for their objectives in the north-western suburbs where they were to take up defensive positions to prevent a

German counter-attack. There was desultory fighting in the town with some Germans, mainly from SS units, feigning death and then shooting at the marines from the rear. This tactic was quickly countered by all 'bodies' being shot as they were passed. Small groups of Germans were also hiding in the ruins of various buildings and one of these fired a *Panzerfaust*, an anti-tank weapon, at 45Cdo's tac HQ, wounding the CO severely in the arm and hitting six members of B Troop with shrapnel. This opposition, however, was quickly overcome and 45Cdo's objective, a large factory, was entered and defensive positions taken up. At dawn the Germans sent out two cycle patrols but both these were quickly eliminated. Then at 1000 hours a fierce counter-attack was launched on E Troop's position on the northern fringe of the factory. Unfortunately, this counter-attack coincided with a ban on artillery support as the XVIIIth US Airborne and the British 6th Airborne were about to land in the area. To make matters worse the Germans had brought up a self-propelled gun to support their attack, and this caused casualties. The troop was eventually given permission to withdraw to better cover further inside the factory, but the troop's commander, Maj Beadle, decided to stay put thus preventing the German infantry which was forming up around the self-propelled gun from entering the factory. Luckily the self-propelled gun withdrew shortly afterwards — probably because the airborne landings required its presence elsewhere — and when the ban on artillery support was lifted an accurate barrage was brought down on the enemy and dispersed them.

At first light that same morning 46Cdo moved into the area and took up defensive

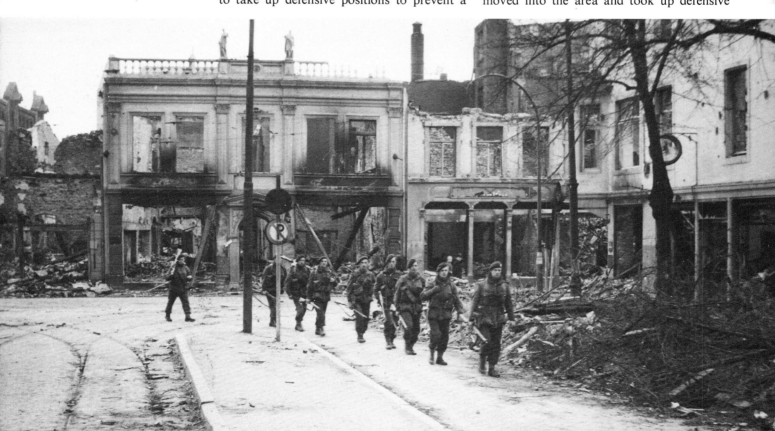

Left: Moving into Wesel. *IWM*

Above: Prisoners captured in Wesel during the fighting were put in a large bomb crater. *IWM*

Right: The German commander, Maj-Gen Deutsch, seen here, was shot dead after refusing to surrender. *IWM*

positions in buildings and a store yard adjacent to 45Cdo. The counter-attacks on their positions were not so severe, though at one point they were heavily shelled by two Tiger tanks which came down the road and hammered away at them for two hours just out of PIAT range. But eventually they withdrew and though German infantry later tried to mount a counter-attack they were dispersed by the Commando's accurate small arms fire. Later American paratroopers began dropping on to the Commando's position and by the afternoon, with the Germans diverted by the airborne landings, the fighting had died down and the night passed quietly apart from some sniping. The next morning a strong fighting patrol was sent out by the CO into Wesel but there was little opposition and 20 prisoners were taken. This brought the brigade's total to 850 since the start of the operation, but considering the intensity of the bombing to which they had been subjected the Germans had put up a stubborn resistance and their commander, Maj-Gen Deutsch, refused to surrender and died with his pistol in his hand.

With Wesel now held by the Allies the Rhine was quickly bridged by engineers — though the Luftwaffe made determined efforts to stop them doing so — and the British 11th Armoured Division swept through the town in hot pursuit of the retreating Germans. So swift was its advance that it bypassed Osnabruck one hundred miles to the east of the Rhine and on 4 April the brigade was ordered to capture it. The assault went in before daylight so as to avoid snipers. Unfortunately for 45Cdo it was light by the time they had reached the sector of the

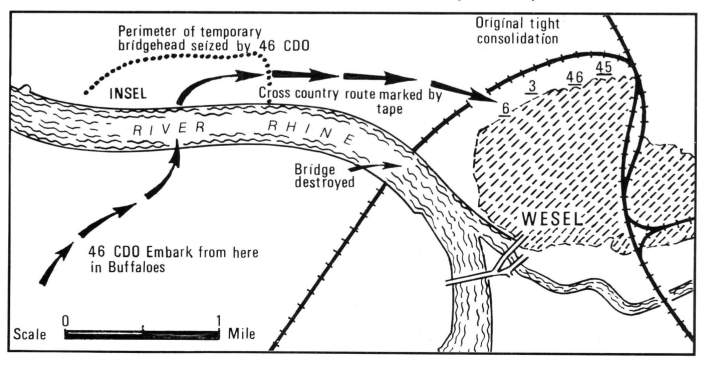

town they were to clear and several casualties occurred. One enemy strongpoint killed Lt Trevor Wright of A Troop as he covered the advance of his section, but the section went forward and stormed the post and annihilated its occupants. Meanwhile, 46Cdo had encountered very light opposition in its section of Osnabruck and by 0800 hours had cleared it. By 1030 hours the whole town, the largest so far captured in Germany by the British, was in the hands of the brigade.

After a brief rest 45Cdo was detached from the rest of the brigade and rushed forward to Stolzenau, a small town on the River Weser. Two infantry companies had established a weak bridgehead on the other side of the Weser and the Commando's task was to pass through them and capture the village of Leese about a mile and a half from the river. As the ground approaching the village was completely flat the plan was to cross the Weser in assault boats and then outflank Leese by moving upstream under cover of the river bank. Leese itself was reported to be defended by two companies of pioneers — not a formidable force.

The crossing was accomplished without many casualties, but once the Commando began to move away from the bridgehead along the eastern bank D Troop which was leading came up against stiff opposition, and there was bitter hand-to-hand fighting. Prisoners from this first encounter soon established that in fact Leese was being defended by an SS training battalion, a rather different proposition from pioneers. Eventually, however, enemy trenches near the landing point were overrun by D Troop

Top left: Members of 'C' Troop, 45Cdo, with trophies captured after the crossing of the Rhine.
RM Archives

Centre left: Members of 46Cdo rounding up prisoners in Osnabruck. *IWM*

Left: Map of Rhine crossing and attack on Wesel.
Reproduced from Commando Men, *by kind permission Bryan Samain*

Above: Marines hoisting their troop flag in Osnabruck. *IWM*

Right: Two marines of 45Cdo on the look-out for snipers in Osnabruck. *IWM*

and then A Troop passed through them and took over the lead. There were some more sharp encounters and at one point the marines set up a Vickers machine gun in the river's shallows and fired it parallel with the bank in an attempt to neutralise the enemy's fire. But this only worked for a short time as the leading troop soon came into its beaten zone and it had to cease firing. 'The tactics for clearing the enemy were very simple,' said Cpl Don Thomas of A Troop, who was one of those out in front. 'We threw a grenade and then rushed in firing madly.' During one of these assaults Thomas was wounded by a stick grenade, but killed the German who had thrown it at him with his American M1 carbine he had been given in Wesel by the airborne troops.

While A Troop were trying to push further along the bank, B Troop and a section of E Troop attempted, by moving up the bed of a stream, to reach a railway embankment which would afford some cover for an attack on the village. It soon became obvious though that the area was much more heavily defended than had been supposed and that the capture of Leese was beyond the capacity of one Commando. 45Cdo was therefore ordered to withdraw to the bridgehead and relieve the two infantry companies. While this was being carried out the Germans launched a counter-attack but this was beaten off by the forward section of B Troop. At dawn the Commando was reinforced and later the rest of the brigade crossed the river. Then in the early hours of the following morning an attack on Leese was launched from the rear, but opposition was negligible as the Germans had already withdrawn.

After a brief rest in Leese and then acting as flank protection to the main divisional advance the brigade moved east again to the next river, the Aller. If the road bridge that spanned this obstacle near the town of Essel could be captured intact the advance of the 11th Armoured Division could continue

unhindered. But a direct assault would certainly have resulted in the bridge being blown so it was decided to cross the Aller by a railway bridge at Schwarmstedt a mile or so downstream from the road bridge and attack it from the enemy's side. This manoeuvre was only partly successful as the railway bridge was blown while the leading units of the brigade were crossing it. But not all the charges went off and this enabled the rest of the brigade to scramble across, and a defensive perimeter was then quickly thrown round the immediate area which was thickly wooded.

When dawn came there were clashes with German patrols from Hademstorf. Then the enemy mounted two strong counter-attacks but both were repulsed, and at 1130 hours one of the army Commandos made a bayonet charge through the woods against the German positions defending the road bridge. They succeeded in clearing the enemy but unfortunately the bridge had already been blown.

The Germans kept up their pressure on the brigade's bridgehead and after 45Cdo's positions had been attacked in the afternoon by tanks as well as by infantry — mainly three battalions of a German marine fusilier regiment — it was realised that the brigade's situation was precarious, and two companies of infantry were sent across to reinforce the Commandos. Though the night passed quietly enough early the next morning the brigade was ordered back to its original positions to clear them of Germans who had infiltrated into them during the night in preparation for a counter-attack. The two Marine Commandos were given this task but 45Cdo's advance was soon held up by fire from their right flank which was coming from a small hill. C Troop was ordered to attack the hill but it came under fire at close range and the troop commander and four others were killed, and four were wounded.

At the same time 46Cdo also came under

Top right: Map of Weser crossing. *Reproduced from* Commando Men, *by kind permission Bryan Samain*

Centre right: Map of Aller crossing and battle. *Reproduced from* Commando Men, *by kind permission Bryan Samain*

Bottom right: German prisoners carrying British wounded into Lauenburg after Elbe crossing. *IWM*

Below: The Elbe crossing begins. *IWM*

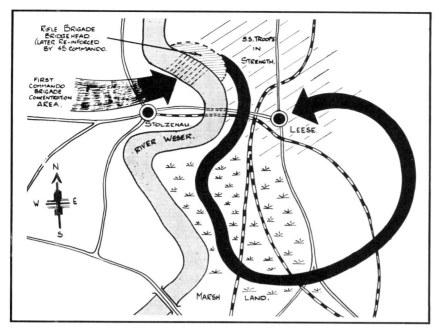

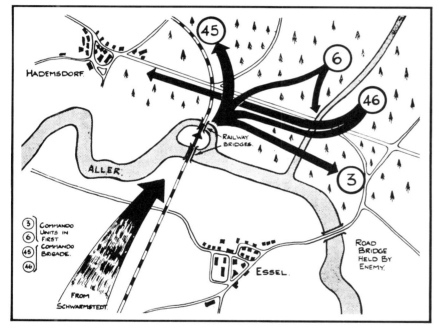

heavy fire and was pinned down, so it was decided both Commandos should withdraw for the night behind a small canal which branched off from the river a few hundred yards downstream from the road bridge. This was accomplished without interference from the enemy, and patrols the following morning reported little enemy activity. At 1100 hours both Commandos, supported by rocket-firing Typhoons, advanced once more and cleared the woods up to their old positions. These were then reoccupied by 45Cdo while 46Cdo, supported by a troop of self-propelled 17-pounder guns, advanced on Hademstorf situated a mile to the west of the railway line. The SP guns were placed on high ground just east of the railway line, and X and Y Troops were sent left-flanking while A and B Troops went to the right. Z Troop was kept in reserve, Y Troop managed to get some men beyond the railway line but were then caught, just as they were entering the woods beyond, by concentrated automatic fire which killed both the troop commander and the troop sergeant-major. Then shortly afterwards one of the section officers was killed and the other was seriously wounded, and, as there were now no officers left, Sgt Cooper took command. With the help of X Troop which had been following up behind he led his men through the woods until they were cleared of Germans.

Meanwhile, on the right flank A and B Troops were able to advance more quickly against lighter opposition and they attacked Hademstorf from the north-east. By this time the enemy's defences were disorganised and, surrounded by marines, they quickly collapsed. 80 prisoners were taken.

The brigade remained in the area for four days guarding the bridge the engineers had built against any possible counter-attack. Then orders came through for the brigade to move, and on 19 April it entered Luneburg, the first infantry to do so. After some days rest there, training began for the crossing of the Elbe ten miles away.

The plan for the Elbe crossing was very similar to that of the Rhine: a heavy bombardment preceding the crossing with the brigade then infiltrating into Lauenburg on the east bank from the rear after skirting the enemy's positions. The bridges across the Elbe-Trave canal were also to be captured. Aerial photographs showed that there were numerous German strongpoints on the high wooded slopes on the east bank of the river but that inland there were few defences. A cross-country route was therefore chosen which would enable an attack on the town from the north to be launched. X Troop, 46Cdo was given the task of taping this route and at 0300 hours they crossed the river ready to pass through the bridgehead already

127

Left: Lt-Col T. M. Gray RM, CO of 46Cdo, being decorated by Field-Marshal Montgomery at Kiel. *IWM*

Below: The German guard of a prison ship at Bremerhaven hands over his rifle to marines of 45Cdo. *IWM*

Bottom: Interrogating a German naval officer at Bremen. *IWM*

established by other units in the brigade. Their landing, however, was not unopposed but was met with small arms fire and some 20mm LAA fire. This did not deter X Troop and it was soon ashore and led by Capt Easton, X Troop commander, climbing the slippery concave-shaped bank which rose to a height of some 150ft, being at its steepest near the top.

The marines were soon spotted and stick grenades began to be thrown down on them from an enemy post at the top of the bank. These caused casualties including the sergeant in charge of the party detailed to tape the route. Capt Easton, realising that the enemy would be outlined against the night sky if he got right under the cliff-top, climbed on up despite the stick grenades. 'Just as I got under the cliff-top,' he said. 'I saw a forearm outlined against the sky above throwing a grenade. It was almost like a traffic policeman directing me where to throw my two grenades at them.' His accurate throwing of his grenades disposed of those in the enemy's post and enabled his troop to climb the bank without any further casualties and to begin taping the way into Lauenburg for the rest of the brigade.

The attack on Lauenburg caught the German garrison totally by surprise, and when 45Cdo entered the town just before dawn B Troop's sergeant-major captured one German who was on his way to wake the cook to make breakfast. By noon the Commando had taken 300 prisoners.

Later the same day 46Cdo moved on the village of Buchhorst to protect the brigade's right flank. It was the last action they were to see before the unconditional surrender of the German Army a few days later. 45Cdo fired their last shots in anger the next day when they were ordered to capture the nearby village of Wangelau which they did after a brief firefight and one casualty. 135 prisoners were taken.

The brigade now moved towards the Baltic ports in the wake of the 11th Armoured Division and the 6th Airborne Division, both of which met virtually no resistance from the disintegrating German Army. Then, on 5 May 1945, all German forces surrendered unconditionally.

One last task remained for the Royal Marines: disarming the German Navy as it returned to the Baltic ports. But this was not carried out by the Marine Commandos but by units of the 116th and 117th Royal Marine Brigades which had been formed from D-Day landing craft personnel when extra infantry was needed in the final push into Germany. They did the job with great dispatch, on one occasion clearing 21 destroyers and two cruisers in one night, and disarming the sometimes truculent crew.